The quick class for typography

CW01500028

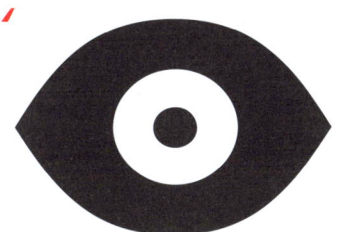

A handbook for designers

Eva Kubinyi et al.

niggli

Contents

2

4

The quick classification guide for typography – A handbook for designers

Next to a selection of more than a hundred relevant typefaces, this book provides essential knowledge about formal, practical, and historical aspects of type. It is supplemented with a complementary web app: www.typ-o.eu

Eva Kubinyi is a graphic designer and professor for typography at the University of Applied Sciences in Aachen, Germany. As a partner at Intégral Ruedi Baur Paris for over 25 years, she conceived and designed major international signage projects for public space and visual identity systems in the cultural field (Swiss Expo.02, celebration of the year 2000 in France, City of Metz, Köln Bonn Airport, Vienna Airport, Grand Paris Express, etc). Eva Kubinyi is member of the DIN committee on 'Schriften'.

Introduction

This essential guide for students, professionals, and occasional type users provides both foundational and advanced knowledge about typefaces. As the constant progress of computer technology triggers the process of type design and generates an overwhelming quantity of thrilling new typefaces, type users require a solid basis in the field of typography. This handbook explains how typefaces are grouped into categories and subcategories, with a focus on the Latin script. The authors present a selection of more than a hundred relevant typefaces, supplemented with historical context, practical information, and explanations of their unique formal characteristics. The goal is to help both regular and occasional users better understand and enhance their use of typography. Key technical terms are explained in the glossary.

The book is supplemented with a web app that contains extensive information and complementary features. Designed as a mobile-first educational website, the app aids in recognizing and classifying typefaces. Rather than automatically identifying individual fonts, its purpose is to teach users how to recognize the underlying formal principles of type design. Check it out: www.typ-o.eu

Eva Kubinyi, Paris & Aachen 2025

www.typ-o.eu
check it out!

next page:
Typeface classifi-
cation by Francis
Thibaudeau,
in: *Manuel français
de typographie
moderne*, Paris,
Bureau de l'Édition,
1924, pp. 108/109
coll. Esad Amiens,
photo: Eva Kubinyi)

Type spreads. The printing revolution dissemi-
nated and democratised texts with the help of
typography. The digital revolution, which is further
accelerating this process, also brings with it
an exponential increase in available fonts.
The topic of font selection is no longer limited to
a professional group of typographers and
designers but has expanded to include the entire
digitally networked society. This handbook
is intended to help font users gain an overview.
Formal contexts, classification principles, and
specialised terminology are explained. After
all, anyone who wants to find their way around
today's font diversity needs some pointers.

The first approach to font classification came
about as a result of Francis Thibaudeau sorting the
font catalogue of the type foundry Peignot & fils.
The diversity of typefaces required a principle
of organisation. In 1924, Thibaudeau proposed
a classification system for text fonts in the Latin
script according to historical epochs and the
shapes of the serifs. The terms and groups he used
can still be found in today's typographic vocabulary,
even if this classification is now outdated. Since
then, there have been numerous approaches to
typeface classification for the Latin script. Official
standards were introduced in the 1960s, but have
not been updated since. Therefore, contemporary
foundries, blogs, or literature about typography
mainly use their own terminology and subdivisions.
In short, there is a certain amount of confusion.

ORIGINE, TRANSFORMATION & CLASSIFICATION
de la
LETTRE D'IMPRIMERIE
DÉTERMINÉES
par son
EMPATTEMENT   La Majuscule.

LES QUATRE GRANDES FAMILLES CLASSIQUES

L'ANTIQUE	**L'ÉGYPTIENNE**	**Le ROMAIN ELZÉVIR**	**Le ROMAIN DIDOT**
TRACÉ PRIMITIF SANS EMPATTEMENT	1ʳᵉ TRANSFORMATION AVEC EMPATTEMENT RECTANGULAIRE	2ᵉ TRANSFORMATION AVEC EMPATTEMENT TRIANGULAIRE	3ᵉ TRANSFORMATION AVEC EMPATTEMENT A TRAIT FIN HORIZONTAL
Relevée sur les inscriptions PHÉNICIENNES et réalisée en types mobiles au commencement du XIXᵉ siècle.	Relevée sur les inscriptions GRECQUES et réalisée en types mobiles au commencement du XIXᵉ siècle.	Relevé sur les inscriptions ROMAINES et réalisé en types mobiles à la fin du XVᵉ siècle.	Principe innové par PHIL. GRANDJEAN et généralisé par F.-A. DIDOT au XVIIIᵉ siècle.
Type de l'*Antique* ou *lettre bâton.*	Type de l'*Égyptienne* à traits bruts.	Type du *romain Garamond* ou *Elzévir.*	Type du *romain Didot.*
ÉGYPTIENNE *Anglaise.*	**Sous-Familles :** Les *ITALIENNES*	**Sous-Familles :** Les *LATINES*	CLASSIQUE DIDOT
Caractéristique : *Arrondissement intérieur des angles d'empattement.*	Caractéristique : *Empattements renforcés. Traits intérieurs amaigris.*	Caractéristique : *Empattement triangulaire horizontal adapté à la graisse de corps de l'Égyptienne angl.*	Caractéristique : *Ajouté d'empattements triangulaires sans modification de la finesse de trait des déliés.*

MONUMENTALES	*Les DE VINNE*	*HELLÉNIQUES*	*TRAITS de PLUME*	*L'AURIOL*
Lettres d'inscriptions, empattements à pointes vives.	*Forme elzévirienne avec exagération des pleins.*	*Traits bi-concaves, empattements triangulaires.*	*Empattements triangulaires au calame.*	*Empattements triangulaires au pinceau.*

ORIGINE, TRANSFORMATION & CLASSIFICATION
de la
LETTRE D'IMPRIMERIE
DÉTERMINÉES
par son

La Minuscule.

EMPATTEMENT

LES QUATRE GRANDES FAMILLES CLASSIQUES

Le ROMAIN ELZÉVIR	Le ROMAIN DIDOT	L'ANTIQUE	L'ÉGYPTIENNE
A EMPATTEMENT *TRIANGULAIRE*	EMPATTEMENT *A TRAIT FIN HORIZONTAL*	SANS EMPATTEMENT	EMPATTEMENT *RECTANGULAIRE*

Le ROMAIN ELZÉVIR — A EMPATTEMENT *TRIANGULAIRE*

Alphabet minuscule extrait de la *Caroline romane* et adapté à l'empattement des capitales romaines d'inscription par Nicolas Jenson à la fin xvᵉ siècle.

Le ROMAIN DIDOT — EMPATTEMENT *A TRAIT FIN HORIZONTAL*

Transformation de la minuscule romaine d'après le principe d'empattement innové par Grandjean dans son *romain du roi* et généralisé par F.-A. Didot au xviiiᵉ siècle.

L'ANTIQUE — SANS EMPATTEMENT

Adoption de la forme romaine de l'alphabet de Nicolas Jenson pour l'ajouté d'une minuscule au type primitif des majuscules phéniciennes.

L'ÉGYPTIENNE — EMPATTEMENT *RECTANGULAIRE*

Adoption de la forme romaine de l'alphabet de Nicolas Jenson pour l'ajouté d'une minuscule aux majuscules des inscriptions grecques.

m — Minuscule *Elzévir*.

m — Minuscule *Didot*.

m — Minuscule *Antique*.

m — Minuscule *Égyptienne*.

Sous-Familles :

Les LATINES

Empattement triangulaire horizontal adapté à la graisse de corps de l'Égyptienne angl. —

CLASSIQUE DIDOT

m — Ajouté d'empattements triangulaires, maintien de la finesse des déliés.

REMARQUE. — Aucun dessin d'alphabet de lettres d'imprimerie ne peut se soustraire à la loi de l'empattement et quel qu'on puisse l'imaginer, il contiendra fatalement dans ses terminaisons de jambages, sa coupe et sa graisse, des éléments-types de classement.

ÉGYPTIENNE Anglaise

m — Arrondissement intérieur des angles d'empattement.

Sous-Famille :

Les ITALIENNES

Les DE VINNE

m — Empattements elzéviriens avec reprises horizontales. —

HELLÉNIQUES

m — Traits bi-concaves, empattements tri-angulaires. —

TRAITS de PLUME

m — Empattements tri-angulaires au calame. —

L'AURIOL

m — Empattements tri-angulaires au pinceau. —

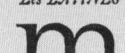

Empattements renforcés; traits intérieurs amaigris.

Type is characterised by conventions. To quote
Zuzana Licko, we read best what we read most.
Even brand-new fonts that are just coming onto the
market always adopt the structures and forms
of existing typefaces. Otherwise, you wouldn't be
able to read them at all. It is therefore possible
to identify common formal characteristics and use
them as the basis for generally valid classifications.
In this book, a classification system based on actual
international terms is used. As a new approach,
we propose a three-level framework: typeface
category, subcategory, and features.

Even if they are not written by hand, many typefaces – especially text typefaces – are formally
influenced by handwriting. They can be differentiated according to their underlying structure.
In text typefaces, one can distinguish between
dynamic, static, and geometric letterforms,
depending on whether the typefaces are close to
Renaissance handwriting (dynamic), or tend to
rationalize forms (static), or even break new ground
in construction (geometric). Recognising this
subdivision requires some practice, but after
a short learning phase it helps to better understand
typographical forms and to better assess the
possible areas of application for the fonts.

As a guide, this publication is made up of chapters
that build on each other. The chapter 'Identify'
enables a step-by-step identification of the formal
characteristics of typefaces. This school of seeing

makes it possible to recognise and name forms and to understand the criteria of typeface classification and areas of use. Especially in the age of artificial intelligence, expertise is important. Directly related to this is the chapter 'Learn', which presents an internationally comprehensible font classification system that conveys the recognisable features of the groups and subgroups, supplemented by historical information and explanations of formal peculiarities.

Type has impact. The immeasurable variety of forms in typography enables a wide range of expressive possibilities. In order to use type appropriately, it is helpful to know prototypical fonts and their areas of application and effect. For this reason, more than 100 relevant fonts are shown and described in more detail in the 'Fonts' chapter. This selection includes important fonts from the history of typography that you should know as a prospective designer or as an interested font user. They were and are often the model for numerous new interpretations (e.g., Garamond, Futura, or Helvetica, to name the best-known examples).

In addition, selected fonts from the digital age are shown, which are representative of the possible variety of forms, concepts, and features (e.g., Noto, a font that aims to support all writing systems of the world in the future). The most important technical terms are explained in the 'Glossary'.

What's in this book?

Identify → page 18
Users of typefaces need knowledge about typeface categories and terminology, in order to be able to determine which font fits to the intended use. The 'Identify' section allows a gradual step-by-step identification of the formal aspects of any typeface.

Learn → page 34
In the 'Learn' section, basic information about how typefaces are grouped into categories and subcategories is presented. This is supplemented there with historical information and explanations of formal particularities.

The classification framework is based on three levels:
→ **Typeface category** (based on terms in international use),
→ **Typeface subcategory** (based on the Principles of Form: Dynamic, Static, and Geometric),
→ **Features** (which have no bearing on the classification, but are quite helpful for describing a typeface). They are described in the 'Glossary', and in the 'Fonts' section.

Fonts A → Z → page 90

The 'Fonts' section shows more than 100 relevant fonts, with detailed descriptions. The selection includes relevant prototypical historic typefaces and contemporary fonts. These examples illustrate and help with understanding typeface classification. The descriptions allow the type-user to understand the semiotic, formal, and technical aspects. Finally, this knowledge helps the user to under-stand the criteria for choosing and making good use of typefaces.

Glossary → page 359

As a discipline, typography has a long history and is in constant progress. Therefore, there is abundant terminology, which can be over-whelming or confusing to students or occasional type-users. All technical terms used in this publication are therefore explained in the glossary. The terms are grouped in sub-chapters: Principles of Form, Character Style, Contrast, General Terms, Letterform Anatomy, Materiality, Technology, and Usage.

100

Sans Serif

Slab Serif

Serif

Display

This publication and the web app www.typ-o.eu use a framework in three levels: **typeface category** (as shown on this page), typeface subcategory, and features.

Handwritten

Blackletter

Overview of
the mobile-first
website:
www.typ-o.eu

Identify

Identify

Users of typefaces need knowledge about typeface categories and terminology, in order to be able to determine which font fits to the indented use. This identify section allows a gradual step-by-step identification of the formal aspects of any typeface.

To determine the category and subcategory a typeface belongs to, take a close look at its general forms.

In the first step, determine whether the typeface is a text typeface, if it is Handwritten, or if it is a Blackletter typeface. If the typeface fits none of these categories, it is probably a Display typeface, continue → page 28

If the typeface to identify is a text typeface, check if it has serifs. For typefaces with serifs, continue → page 22 For typefaces without serifs, continue → page 24 You need to determine some more aspects before getting to the final result.

If the typeface to identify is a Handwritten typeface, determine whether the strokes are connected or interrupted. (→ Learn, page 72) For the final result, continue → page 32

If the typeface to identify is a Blackletter typeface, determine which subcategory it belongs to. These subcategories follow historical classifications. (→ Learn, page 78) For the final result, continue → page 32

With Serifs → Arnhem

Akiem

Without Serifs → Gotham

Verena

Handwritten → Brush Script

Blackletter → Unger Fraktur

Serifs are the concluding horizontal flicks at the end of a typeface's strokes.

Serifs can be divided into three groups based on their general form and stroke thickness: serifs that are as thin as the typeface's hairlines, tapering 'wedge-shaped' serifs and serifs as thick as the typeface's stems. Furthermore, serifs can differ in terms of how they transition from a typeface's stems.

Take a close look at the forms of the serifs. Even if they don't necessarily determine the typeface's classification, they give information about the formal and historic models of the typeface.

After you have examined the serifs, continue to the next page.

Sibylle

Firmin

Peter

The **Stroke Contrast** (also referred to simply as contrast, or stroke-thickness contrast) describes the difference between a typeface's thick and thin strokes.

Take a close look at the stroke contrast. After you have determined the contrast, continue to the next page.

High stroke contrast can be found in Static Serif typefaces like Didot. The difference between thick (vertical) and thin (horizontal) strokes is important.

Low stroke contrast can often (but not exclusively) be found in dynamic typefaces.

Some typefaces have no perceivable stroke contrast, like most Geometric Sans Serif typefaces, for example. With reverse contrast, the conventional distribution of the thick and thin strokes is switched around.

Martin

Zuzana

Alisa

Lara

The **Formal Principle** is the basic principle of design underlying the character of a typeface. It influences a typeface's impact and legibility. (→ Learn, pages 40, 50, 60)

Typefaces with a **Dynamic Principle of Form** are formally related to letterforms that were written with a broad pen. They have a diagonal contrast axis and their in-strokes are usually diagonal as well. The letterforms are differentiated from one another and open ('a', 'c', 'e', and 's').

Typefaces with a **Static Principle of Form** are related to letterforms that are written with a pointed pen. They have a vertical contrast axis and their in-strokes are usually horizontal. The letterforms seem to have a symmetrical construction and are closed ('a', 'c', 'e', and 's').

Typefaces based on the **Geometric Principle of Form** look constructed. Their texture is determined by straight lines and curved circle-segments.

There are also typefaces that are not constructed according to the Dynamic, Static or Geometric Principles of Form.

To determine the subcategory a typeface belongs to, take a close look at the contruction of the letterforms. Continue to the next page.

Dynamic Principle of Form → Garamond

Roger

Static Principle of Form → Helvetica

Roxane

Geometric Principle of Form → Futura

Adrian

Informal → Lÿno Jean

Typefaces can be differentiated according to other features.

Though they have no bearing on the classification by category and subcategory, they can determine the typefaces' visual aspect and area of use.

Take a close look at the features of the typeface to identify, for instance:

→ **Glyph Style:**
monolinear, monospace, proportional, rotated, rounded, unterlined, unicase.
→ **Materiality:**
dot matrix, inscription, pixel typeface, stencil typeface, typewriter.
→ **Technology:**
random font, screen font, SIL OFL, variable font.
→ **Usage:**
caption, multi-script typeface, newspaper typeface, super family, text typeface, titling typeface.

Find definitions in the → Glossary, page 359

Continue to the next page to check out the results.

Monospace → IBM Plex Mono

Herb

Unicase → New Alphabet

Pixel Typeface → Lo-Res

Lucas

Stencil Typeface → Cargo

Jan

Serif
→ Learn, page 38

Slab Serif
→ Learn, page 48

Dynamic Serif
→ Sample: Sabon

Dynamic Slab Serif
→ Sample: Caecilia

Roxane

Roxane

Static Serif
→ Sample: Didot Elder

Static Slab Serif
→ Sample: Clarendon

Roxane

Roxane

Serif typefaces have wedge-shaped or hairline-weight serifs, for example.

Geometric Slab Serif
→ Sample: Rockwell

Roxane

Slab Serif typefaces have stem-weight serifs and generally low (or no) stroke contrast.

Sans Serif
→ Learn, ^{page 58}

Dynamic Sans Serif
→ Sample: Fedra Sans

Roxane

Static Sans Serif
→ Sample: Helvetica

Roxane

Geometric Sans Serif
→ Sample: Futura

Roxane

As a result of the step-by-step identification, this chart shows the main categories and subcategories.

The main categories for text typefaces are: **Serif, Slab Serif, Sans Serif.**

The subcategories are based on the **Principles of Form**. For example, a text typeface with stem-weight serifs and Static Formal Principle is a **Static Slab Serif** typeface.

Stroke contrast and features like glyph style, materiality, technology, or usage are important additional characteristics, as they can determine the typeface's visual aspect and area of use. They are not included in these charts, as they are too numerous.

Display
→ Learn, page 70

Handwritten
→ Learn, page 72

→ Sample: Orientation

Script (connected)
→ Sample: Mistral

Roxane

Roxane

Typefaces with free and unique forms that primarily serve decorative purposes are called Display typefaces. Although these typefaces are mainly based on the same letterforms as the Serif and the Sans Serif, their decorative character is the focus.

Graphic (interrupted)
→ Sample: Comic Sans

Roxane

The lack of binding classification features in Display typefaces makes a clear division into sub-categories almost impossible.

Blackletter
→ Learn, page 78

Textura
→ Sample: Old English

Roxane

Fraktur
→ Sample: Fette Fraktur

Roxane

Rotunda
→ Sample: San Marco

Roxane

Blackletter Variations
→ Sample: Eskapade

Roxane

Bastarda
→ Sample: Alte Schwabacher

Roxane

Learn

Learn

Serif → 38

Subcategories:
Dynamic Serif
Transitional Serif
Static Serif
Geometric Serif

Slab Serif → 48

Subcategories:
Dynamic Slab Serif
Static Slab Serif
Geometric Slab Serif

Sans Serif → 58

m

Subcategories:
Dynamic Sans Serif
Transitional Sans Serif
Static Sans Serif
Geometric Sans Serif

This classification system is based on various existing terms and group divisions. The groups on the left page are mainly text typefaces (Serif, Slab Serif, Sans Serif). The groups on the right page are useful for short texts, big scale, and strong expressions.

Display → 70

Handwritten → 72

Subcategories:
Script *(connected)*
Graphic *(interrupted)*

Blackletter → 78

Subcategories:
Textura
Rotunda
Bastarda
Fraktur
~ Variations

Serif

EN	**Serif**
DE	**Serifenschrift** (*Antiqua*)
FR	**Sérif** (*Caractère à empattement*)

m

m

**Typefaces with serifs and different stroke
thicknesses are often described as Serif.
Some typefaces, especially those with stroke
contrast, have serifs. The term 'Serif' is
a little ambiguous. Here, it is primarily used to
separate this category from the Sans Serif
and the Slab Serif groups.**

Historical Background

From a historical perspective, the typefaces
we use today originate from the so-called 'roman'.
The letterforms are based on the Humanistic
minuscule and the majuscules of the Capitalis
Monumentalis used by the Ancient Romans.
The first typefaces of this kind arose under

the influence of Humanism at the time of the Renaissance in the 15th century, at first in Italy and later in France. Additional forms were developed during the 17th and 18th centuries. The latter of those variants is characterised above all by more extreme stroke contrast and the increasing loss of the dynamic letterforms inspired by writing.

Disambiguation

In typography, the expression 'roman' originally described the rounded-arched letterforms of Roman origin, differentiated from Blackletter styles. The corresponding German term 'Antiqua' grew out of the Renaissance 'lettera antiqua' – a style of handwriting supposedly based on a model from antiquity. However, the reference point for the lower-case letters was not a writing style used by the Romans, but rather the Carolingian minuscule used in Charlemagne's time for copying classical texts. The term 'Serif' refers to the concluding horizontal flicks or 'feet' at the end of a typeface's strokes. Its name probably comes from the Dutch word *schreef*, for stroke or line. In today's context, the term 'Serif' is often applied to the group of Serif typefaces with stroke contrast, as opposed to Sans Serif and Slab Serif.

Subcategories

→ Dynamic Serif, Transitional Serif, Static Serif, Geometric Serif

Dynamic Serif

→ page 42

Transitional Serif

→ page 44

Static Serif

→ page 46

Geometric Serif

Dynamic Principle of Form: The letters are fully differentiated from each other, and their dependence on Humanistic handwriting styles is noticeable. The letterforms are open. These typefaces are suitable for longer texts intended for immersive reading.

Transition from the Dynamic to the Static Principle of Form: The letterforms are more rationally coordinated with one another than in earlier Serif typefaces. There is a tendency toward the standardisation of stroke-endings and serifs.

Static Principle of Form: The letterforms appear constructed, the underlying principle of rational construction is recognisable. The forms of the lower-case letters are closed. These typefaces are less suitable as text typefaces.

In theory, the Geometric Principle of Form can apply to Serif typefaces. As this this subcategory is quite rare, it is not included in this publication.

Dynamic Serif

EN	**Dynamic Serif** *(Humanistic, Old Style)*
DE	**Dynamische Serifenschrift** *(Renaiss.-Antiqua)*
FR	**Sérif dynamique** *(Humane, Garalde)*

→ Sample: Garamond

Whenever the black fox jumped the squirrel gazed suspiciously.

The Dynamic Serif is characterised by the stroke movement used in Humanistic handwriting styles, which comes from writing with a broad pen held at a fixed, slanted angle in relation to the baseline.

Historical Background

The Dynamic Serif originated in Venice. During the Renaissance, the first typefaces in this style were created there around 1470, which were later developed further in France. Beginning after 1530, the Parisian punchcutter and typefounder Claude Garamont designed a new style of typeface, which because of its formal qualities and its excellent reading properties quickly developed into a valid standard. Typefaces from this category are still used today, especially for longer texts intended for immersive reading.

Formal Principle, Contrast Axis

Dynamic Principle of Form: The letters are fully differentiated from each other, and their dependence on Humanistic handwriting styles is noticeable. The letterforms are open (especially 'a', 'c', and 'e'). The stroke contrast is less pronounced than in other Serif subcategories. The contrast axis of the round letters (like 'o' and 'e') is inclined to the left.

Other Features

The in-strokes and top serifs are often slanted, the transition from the serifs to the stem is often rounded (bracketed). The lower-case 'g' is usually double-storey. The upper-case letters are based on the proportions of the Capitalis Monumentalis.

Hamburg

Transitional Serif

EN	**Transitional Serif** *(Realist)*
DE	**Übergangs-Serifenschrift** *(Barock-Antiqua)*
FR	**Sérif de transition** *(Réale)*

→ Sample: Baskerville

Whenever the black fox jumped the squirrel gazed suspiciously.

Typefaces that mix the formal characteristics of the Dynamic and the Static Serif in various ways are described as Transitional Serifs. The Humanistic forms of the Dynamic Serif became increasingly more static. They no longer followed the original movement of the broad pen, the letters became more rationally coordinated with each other. The typefaces in this category have more contrast than their predecessors.

Historical Background

As the name suggests, the transitions between the Dynamic Serif and the Transitional Serif are fluid. The first typefaces influenced by pointed-pen calligraphy and copperplate engraving were created during the height of the baroque, beginning around 1700. Attempts to construct letters on paper and advances in printing technology accompanied this development. The transitional phase for Serif typefaces reached its conclusion with the English typefaces of the 18th century. John Baskerville and William Caslon are among the most well-known type designers from this era.

Formal Principle, Contrast Axis

Transition from the Dynamic to the Static Principle of Form: The letterforms are more rationally coordinated with one another than in earlier Serif typefaces. There is a tendency toward the standardisation of stroke-endings and serifs. The stroke contrast is more pronounced than in Dynamic Serif typefaces. The contrast axis of the round letters (such as 'o' and 'e') inclines slightly to the left or is vertical.

Other Features

Often, the in-strokes and serifs are almost straight. Serifs are more likely to consistently be placed at right angles to the stem, the transitions are bracketed more strongly. In many of this category's typefaces, the leg of the upper-case 'R' is diagonal and the foot of the leg stands firmly on the baseline.

Static Serif

EN	**Static Serif** (*Modern, Rational*)
DE	**Statische Serifenschrift** (*Klassiz. Antiqua*)
FR	**Sérif statique** (*Didone*)

→ Sample: Didot Elder

Whenever the black fox jumped the squirrel gazed suspiciously.

Characteristic for the Static Serifs is the high contrast between the stem and the hairline as well as the symmetrical distribution of stroke contrast.

Historical Background

The first typefaces of this kind emerged at the beginning of the neoclassical period, starting around 1770 and they embody the rational thought at the time of the Enlightenment. Important type designers from this era include, among others, the Italian Giambattista Bodoni and the Frenchman François Ambroise Didot. Their eponymous typefaces became the most popular Serif typefaces in neoclassical Europe. Due to their characters' high contrast and symmetry, these typefaces are less suitable as text typefaces, and today they are used for headlines and large-size applications.

Formal Principle, Contrast Axis

Static Principle of Form: The letterforms appear constructed, the underlying principle of rational construction is recognisable. The forms of the lower-case letters are closed. The stroke contrast is very clear and sometimes extreme. The contrast axis of the round letters is vertical.

Other Features

The delicate serifs are horizontal and stand firmly on the baseline. The serifs are often straight or set at right angles to the stem. The lower-case letters 'a', 'r', and 'f' usually have teardrop-shaped terminals. The leg of the upper-case 'R' is often curved and is almost vertical. For most typefaces in this subcategory, the proportions of the characters are standardised and the upper-case letters have similar widths.

Hamburg

Slab Serif

EN	**Slab Serif**	(*Egyptienne*)
DE	**Serifenbetonte Schrift**	(*Egyptienne*)
FR	**Mécane**	(*Égyptienne*)

Typefaces with strongly distinct, accentuated serifs and predominantly consistent stroke thicknesses are called Slab Serif. The transition to Serif typefaces is fluid, especially for newspaper typefaces, which have enhancements to their contrast and serifs. Their usually low stroke contrast is also reminiscent of the linear Sans Serif typefaces.

Historical Background

The Slab Serif originated during the era of industrialisation in response to the increased need for robust newspaper typefaces and flamboyant advertising typefaces. The first typefaces of this kind were developed in England at the beginning of the 19th century. The Static Serif served as a pattern at first, and its stroke thickness was made uniform. This resulted in typefaces with strong serifs. The further development of the Slab Serif based on geometric construction ran parallel with the creation of Sans Serif typefaces.

Disambiguation

The terms 'Egyptienne' were informed by the Egyptomania that Napoleon Bonaparte's Egyptian campaign had set off at the beginning of the 19th century. In English, this category is more often referred to by the term 'Slab Serif', which refers to the thick, usually rectangular form of the serifs that typefaces in this group have. The typefaces themselves have no formal connection to Egypt, however some authors have suggested that the slab-like serifs have visual parallels with shapes used in Ancient Egyptian architecture.

Subcategories

→ Dynamic Slab Serif, Static Slab Serif, Geometric Slab Serif

Dynamic Slab Serif → page 52

Static Slab Serif → page 54

Geometric Slab Serif → page 56

Dynamic Principle of Form: The letterforms are open or pronounced. It is noticeable that their construction has its origin in handwriting. The contrast axis of the round letters inclines diagonally to the left. These typefaces are suitable for longer texts intended for immersive reading.

Static Principle of Form: The letterforms are closed; the underlying principle of rational construction can be recognised. Stroke contrast is usually not visible. The contrast axis of the round letters tends to be vertical. These typefaces are less suitable as text typefaces.

Geometric Principle of Form: The letters' construction is based on simple geometric shapes (triangle, circle and square). Stroke contrast can usually not be recognised. Due to their severely constructed letterforms, these typefaces are only of limited use as text typefaces.

Dynamic Slab Serif

EN	**Dynamic Slab Serif** *(Humanistic ~)*
DE	**Dynamische Serifenbetonte**
FR	**Mécane dynamique**

→ Sample: Caecilia

Whenever the black fox jumped the squirrel gazed suspiciously.

The Dynamic Slab Serif, in contrast to the Static and Geometric Slab Serif, is characterised by more open forms. It takes up the Humanistic stroke pattern of the Dynamic Serif and usually has a light, but visible stroke contrast.

Historical Background

Until about 1990, Eric Gill's Joanna was practically the only typeface that one could assign to this subcategory. Only with the design of Caecilia from Peter Matthias Noordzij did the previously static Slab Serif typefaces become increasingly more dynamic. To be able to use Slab Serif typefaces for body text as well, the first Dynamic Slab Serif typefaces with Humanistic features and properties to optimise reading were created.

Formal Principle, Contrast Axis

Dynamic Principle of Form: The letterforms are open or pronounced. It is noticeable that their construction has its origin in handwriting.
A light degree of stroke contrast is recognisable, and the contrast axis of the round letters (like 'o' and 'e') inclines diagonally to the left.

Other Features

The serifs are often set straight or at a right angle to the stem. The minuscule 'a' and 'g' are usually double-storey. The leg of the upper-case 'R' is usually diagonal.

Hamburg

Static Slab Serif

EN **Static Slab Serif** *(Rational ~)*
DE **Statische Serifenbetonte**
FR **Mécane statique**

→ Sample: Karloff Neutral

Whenever the black fox jumped the squirrel gazed suspiciously.

The Static Slab Serif is based on the character of the Static Serif, but in contrast to this, it has pronounced serifs and uniform stroke thickness.

Historical Background

The first Slab Serif typefaces originated at the beginning of the Industrial Revolution in England, towards the end of neoclassicism (1760–1830). Therefore, they can be understood as a kind of further development for the Static Serif, whose Formal Principle they adopted. Initially, they still looked like severely fattened-up Serif typefaces, with clear and distinctly-emphasised serifs only intended for use in large sizes (e.g., for advertising). Over the 19th century, the Static Slab Serif developed from a purely decorative typeface into a robust text typeface and became the model for many newspaper typefaces. Typefaces in this group are still used today, but they are not as easy to read in body text as Dynamic Slab Serif typefaces.

Formal Principle, Contrast Axis

Static Principle of Form: The letterforms are closed; the underlying principle of rational construction can be recognised. Stroke contrast is usually not visible. The contrast axis of the round letters (like 'o' and 'e') tends to be vertical.

Other Features

The serifs are generally at right angles or they are set straight up against the stems. The 'Clarendon' typeface is an exception since the transitions from serifs to the stem are bracketed there. The lower-case letters 'a', 'g', and 'r' sometimes have teardrop-shaped terminals. The leg of the upper-case 'R' is partially curved; in the Clarendon typeface, this tail is particularly distinctive.

Hamburg

Geometric Slab Serif

→ Sample: Rockwell

Whenever the black fox jumped the squirrel gazed suspiciously.

The Geometric Slab Serif corresponds formally to the Geometric Sans Serif. In contrast to this, however, it has very pronounced serifs that are as thick as the stems.

Historical Background

The first Slab Serif typefaces of this kind were created around 1930 as a result of the Geometric Sans Serif typefaces that had already been developed, which had also been constructed with a ruler and compass. Due to their severely constructed letterforms, these typefaces are only of limited use as text typefaces.

Hamburg

Sans Serif

EN   **Sans Serif** (*Grotesque, Gothic*)
DE   **Serifenlose** (*Grotesk, Linear-Antiqua*)
FR   **Linéale** (*Sans sérif*)

Typefaces without serifs whose formal principles come from the Serif categories are called Sans Serif. Many typefaces in this group have very little or no stroke contrast. However, there are some typefaces that do have obvious stroke contrast, especially among contemporary typefaces.

Historical Background

Like the Slab Serif, the Sans Serif came into being at the end of neoclassicism in England. The emergence of advertising at the beginning of the 19th century favoured the creation of large eye-catching typefaces. The Serif typefaces that were predominant at that time had their serifs removed, which would have been hardly imaginable up until that point. Initially only used as a headline typeface for posters and advertisements, the Sans Serif became popular as a text typeface for longer documents in the 20th century.

Disambiguation

The first typefaces from this category were perceived as being 'grotesque' because their Sans Serif form was so unusual. In English, Sans Serif is the most commonly used term now, but Grotesque has long been popular, too – especially in the UK – with Gothic also being a common term for Sans Serif in the US.

Subcategories

→ Dynamic Sans Serif, Transitional Sans Serif, Static Sans Serif, Geometric Sans Serif

Dynamic Sans Serif

→ page 62

Transitional Sans Serif

→ page 64

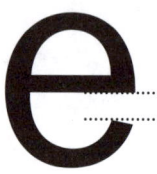

Static Sans Serif

→ page 66

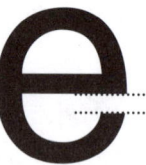

Geometric Sans Serif

→ page 68

Dynamic Principle of Form: The letterforms are open or pronounced. Their handwritten origins are noticeable in their construction. The stroke contrast is usually low. Due to its friendly-looking calligraphic ductus and its good legibility, the Dynamic Sans Serif's areas of use are versatile.

Typefaces that fall into the Transitional Sans Serif group have a Formal Principle constructed in a way that looks like the Static Sans Serif. However, narrow and open letterforms benefiting legibility are a Transitional Sans Serif characteristic, too.

Static Principle of Form: The letterforms are even (or almost even) and are closed in on themselves. Their stroke contrast is usually less than in Transitional Sans Serifs. These typefaces are less suitable as text typefaces.

Geometric Principle of Form: The letters are extremely reduced. Their construction is based on geometric shapes and they all look very similar to one another. The stroke contrast is usually low. Due to the their very constructed letterforms, these typefaces are less suitable for use in body text.

Dynamic Sans Serif

EN	**Dynamic Sans Serif** *(Humanistic ~)*
DE	**Dynamische Serifenlose**
FR	**Linéale dynamique**

→ Sample: Gill Sans

Whenever the black fox jumped the squirrel gazed suspiciously.

The formal principle of the Dynamic Sans Serif references the broad-nib characteristics of the Dynamic Serif. Therefore, it seems more organic and less constructed than the Static Sans Serif.

Historical Background

The first examples from this subcategory emerged during the revival of Humanistic-style Serif type-faces in early-20th century Britain. The Johnston typeface – named after its designer Edward Johnston – was developed in 1916 for the London Underground and is considered a prototype for the development of the Dynamic Sans Serif. Its intro-duction influenced several later Sans Serif typefaces from the 1920s. In particular, Gill Sans (1928) from the British type designer Eric Gill, who had also been involved with Johnston's development. Due to its friendly-looking calligraphic ductus and its good legibility, the Dynamic Sans Serif's areas of use are versatile.

Formal Principle, Contrast Axis

Dynamic Principle of Form: The letterforms are open or pronounced. Their handwritten origins are noticeable in their construction. The stroke contrast is usually low. However, there are type-faces with visible stroke contrast. The contrast axis of round letters (like 'o' und 'e') inclines to the left.

Other Features

The lower-case 'a' and 'g' are usually double-storey. The leg of the capital 'R' is usually diagonal.

Hamburg

Transitional Sans Serif

EN **Transitional Sans Serif** (*American Gothic*)
DE **Übergangs-Serifenlose** (*Amerik. Grotesk*)
FR **Linéale de transition**

→ Sample: Franklin Gothic

Whenever the black fox jumped the squirrel gazed suspiciously.

Typefaces that fall into the Transitional Sans Serif group have a Formal Principle constructed in a way that looks like the Static Sans Serif. However, narrow and open letterforms benefiting legibility are a Transitional Sans Serif characteristic, too.

Historical Background

The Transitional Sans Serif was primarily developed in the United States, which is why it is often called the 'American Gothic'. The first typefaces of this kind were already created in the middle of the 19th century – at the same time as the Static Sans Serif's predecessors. However, Transitional Sans Serifs became popular in the early 20th century, especially when they began to be used in newspaper printing. One of the best-known representatives of this category is Franklin Gothic, designed by Morris Fuller Benton at the American Type Founders Co. (ATF) shortly after the turn of the century.

Formal Principle, Contrast Axis

The letters are narrow and the x-height is correspondingly large. Letterforms are open and clearly defined. The stroke contrast is usually low. However, there are also typefaces with more explicit stroke contrast. The contrast axis of round letters (like 'o' and 'e') is vertical or slightly inclined to the left.

Other Features

The lower-case 'a' and 'g' are usually double-storey. The leg of the capital 'R' is usually diagonal and has a curled foot. The capital 'G' usually has a spur.

Hamburg

Static Sans Serif

EN	**Static Sans Serif** (*Neo-grotesque ~*)
DE	**Statische Serifenlose**
FR	**Linéale statique**

→ Sample: Helvetica

Whenever the black fox jumped the squirrel gazed suspiciously.

Letters with a uniform construction are a typical feature of the Static Sans Serif. They are closed in on themselves and their proportions are inspired by the Static Serif.

Historical Background

The predecessors of the Static Sans Serif were created during the 19th century. These include Akzidenz Grotesk, which was designed around the turn of the century (1898). Originally designed as a headline typeface, it is considered the proto-type for Static Sans Serif typefaces and it influenced the aesthetic of many other typefaces from this category. The peak of the Static Sans Serif's development was in the 1950s and 1960s.

One of the most important examples of this style is the Helvetica typeface, which was designed in 1957 by Max Miedinger and Eduard Hoffmann in Switzerland.

Formal Principle, Contrast Axis

Static Principle of Form: The letterforms are even (or almost even) and are closed in on themselves. Their stroke contrast is usually less than in Transitional Sans Serifs. However, there are also typefaces with more explicit stroke contrast. The contrast axis of the round letters (like 'o' and 'e') is vertical.

Other Features

The lower-case 'a' is usually double-storey, yet the 'g' is single-storey. The capital letters all have similar widths. The leg of the capital 'R' is usually either diagonal or vertical with a curled foot.

Hamburg

Geometric Sans Serif

EN	**Geometric Sans Serif**
DE	**Geometrische Serifenlose**
FR	**Linéale géométrique**

→ Sample: Futura

Whenever the black fox jumped the squirrel gazed suspiciously.

The Geometric Sans Serif is particularly characterised by its strongly reduced, uniform letters. Their forms are strictly constructed and based on geometric shapes.

Historical Background

The first Geometric Sans Serif typefaces were developed in Germany under the influence of the functionalism of the 1920s. The functionalist idea of the Bauhaus movement called for new, extremely simplified typographic forms. Through to the present day, the most well-known and beloved example of this subcategory is Futura (1927) from Paul Renner. In addition to its typically Geometric Principle of Form, it is particularly characterised by its extremely even stroke thickness. Due to the their very constructed letterforms, Geometric Sans Serifs are less suitable for use in body text.

Formal Principle, Contrast Axis

Geometric Principle of Form: The letters are extremely reduced. Their construction is based on geometric shapes (triangle, circle, and square) and they all look very similar to one another. The stroke contrast is usually low.

Other Features

The lower-case 'a' is usually single-storey.

Display

EN	**Display** *(Headline typeface)*
DE	**Schauschrift** *(Titelschrift, Zierschrift)*
FR	**Caractère de titrage** *(~ décoratif)*

Typefaces with free and unique forms that primarily serve decorative purposes are called Display typefaces. Although these typefaces are mainly based on the same letterforms as the Serif and the Sans Serif, their decorative character is the focus.

Disambiguation

The English-language terms 'Display typeface' or 'Headline typeface' indicate their use in headlines and large-format applications. The term 'Display typeface' is not to be confused with screen typefaces.

Subcategories

As a rule, Display typefaces are not suitable for use in body text and are usually used in large type sizes common for titles or short texts. Due to their widely varying formal properties and the lack of binding classification features, they cannot easily be sorted, which makes a clear division into subcategories almost impossible.

→ Samples: Dot Matrix, Blur

Handwritten

The Handwritten typefaces group comprises typefaces that have a clear written character and whose shapes are strongly influenced by their respective writing tool.

Disambiguation

Handwritten typefaces, like italic typefaces, are derived from handwriting. This Handwritten typefaces group includes examples with independent forms. By contrast, italic typefaces do not form a specific classification category. They usually have an accompanying function and are assigned to typefaces from other categories.

Fiona

→ Sample: Bello Script

Script (connected)

EN	**Script**
DE	**Schreibschrift**
FR	**Scripte**

→ Sample: Mistral

Whenever the black fox jumped the squirrel gazed suspiciously.

The Script subcategory includes typefaces based on the calligraphic character of handwriting. The historical models, so-called vernacular styles, were mainly used in correspondence. In contrast to the Graphic typefaces, the letters in most Script typefaces are connected so that it seems as if whole words were written in one go.

Historical Background

Individual handwriting styles and calligraphic models from before and after the invention of printing serve as the basis for printed Script typefaces. The shapes and stroke patterns of Script typefaces are strongly influenced by the writing tools used in the respective handwritten models (e. g., pen, brush, chalk, etc.). Because of their difficult legibility, Script typefaces are generally not suitable for longer amounts of text and are often only used for headlines or to serve a decorative purpose.

Attributes

Handwritten character, letters written in one go.

Hamburg

Graphic (interrupted)

EN   **Graphic**
DE   **Handschriftliche Druckschrift** (~ *Antiqua*)
FR   **Manuaire**

→ Sample: Comic Sans

Whenever the black fox jumped the squirrel gazed suspiciously.

The Graphic subcategory includes typefaces whose letterforms may be reminiscent of Serif or Sans Serif typefaces, but which nevertheless have a distinctively handwritten character. Their historical models are handwritten book typefaces. The individual letters of these typefaces are usually not connected.

Historical Background

Typefaces from this subcategory are based on roman printing types with curved arches. The formative character of the respective writing tools (e. g., pen, brush, chalk, etc.) is quite clear in Graphic typefaces. Although these typefaces are often more readable than Script typefaces, they are generally not suited for use in body text and are used primarily for headlines or decorative purposes instead.

Attributes

Handwritten character; a handwritten alphabet adapted in a personal manner.

Blackletter

Typefaces whose letters' arches are broken in whole or in part are called Blackletter. They are opposites of typefaces with curved arches – a description that is equally applicable for Serif, Sans Serif, and Slab Serif typefaces.

Historical Background

Blackletter writing styles originated during the High Middle Ages. Influenced by writing with the broad pen, the Gothic minuscule developed out of the Carolingian minuscule. In turn, that handwriting style is considered to have been the basis for the first typefaces, which shaped printing in Northern Europe for several centuries. Particularly in Germany, Fraktur remained popular

into the 20th century. In Southern Europe
– especially in Italy and France – a turn toward
Serif type was already taking place at the end of the
15th century.

Disambiguation

The English name for this category refers to how
dark its letterforms often appear on the page.
Blackletter typefaces often have strokes that are
closer together than is common in roman typefaces.
Also in Blackletter, the upper-case letters are
often made up of more strokes than their roman
counterparts. Both of these features reduce
the amount of non-printing 'white space' inside the
letterforms, and as a result, a lot of black ink was
historically printed on the page (i.e., blackletter).
In Great Britain, Blackletter was often called
'Gothic'. That is not the best name for Blackletter
types, as Sans Serif typefaces were also tradition-
ally referred to in the United States with the term
'Gothic.'

Subcategories

→ Textura, Rotunda, Bastarda, Fraktur,
Blackletter Variations

→ Sample: Old English

Whenever the black fox jumped the squirrel gazed suspiciously.

The name Textura refers to the texture-like character of the narrow texture that is a typical feature of this letterform style, reminiscent of woven fabrics.

Historical Background

Created during the 14th century, Textura grew out of the Early Gothic minuscule. Originally used as a handwriting style for book text, Textura developed alongside the invention of printing (around 1450) to become the first printed typeface and the prototype for typography. In 1454, it was used by Johannes Gutenberg for the printing of his 42-line bible and then established itself in Germany as the leading style for printed religious

Latin texts. The calligraphic influences from its handwritten predecessors were still clearly visible in printed Textura typefaces.

Attributes

The letters are narrow and high-reaching. At the same time, the stems of the minuscules are broken. The in-strokes and out-strokes are often diamond or cube-shaped. Decorative majuscules are a characteristic feature.

Rotunda

→ Sample: San Marco

Whenever the black fox jumped the squirrel gazed suspiciously.

Like Textura, Rotunda follows a typical stroke pattern of the broad pen. However, its forms are simpler, rounder and less broken than in Textura.

Historical Background

Rotunda developed as an alternative form of Textura in Southern Europe. Especially in Italy and Spain, Blackletter styles arose in the early years of printing that took up Textura's Gothic Principle of Form, but whose letters nevertheless had curves. For this reason, Rotunda is often referred to as a 'Round Gothic'. Rotunda was used especially for academic and legal texts in Latin. At the beginning of the 16th century, Rotunda was largely replaced by the emerging Renaissance typefaces. In Italy it remained in use into the 17th century.

Attributes

The letters have simpler, rounder forms than in Textura. Tight curves and no breaking can be seen. The majuscules are not as decorative as with Textura. There are no diamond or cube-shaped in-strokes and out-strokes.

Bastarda

→ Sample: Alte Schwabacher

Whenever the black fox jumped the squirrel gazed suspiciously.

Bastarda is a further development of the Gothic Textura combining an Italic design language with elements of calligraphic book handwriting styles. Its texture is open and runs wide, its letters are mostly rounder than in Textura or Fraktur.

Historical Background

Bastarda was the writing style used most often during the Middle Ages. The name Bastarda refers to its place between handwriting and book-copying styles. Rapid handwriting speeds caused changes to appear in the shapes of Textura, which lead to many regional Bastardas. The Late Gothic Schwabacher Bastarda, one of the most legible Gothic writing styles, was developed during the second half of the 15th century. It first appeared in Southern Germany and became the main vernacular text and book-copying style for the German language before it was largely replaced by Fraktur. With the use of the Wittenberg Bastarda as the typeface in the Luther Bible, the Bastarda acquired a particular historical relevance that continues to this day.

Attributes

The letters have round and broken forms, although the curves are wider than they are in Rotunda. Fundamentally, the overall impression is lighter, because the letters' interior spaces are wider. The lower-case 'g' has a strong horizontal stroke, while the capital 'H' and 'S' have unusual forms.

Fraktur

→ Sample: Fette Fraktur

Whenever the black fox jumped the squirrel gazed suspiciously.

Fraktur emerged as a further development of the Schwabacher Bastarda and it is also based on the broken stroke pattern of the broad pen, which it combines with curved forms.

Historical Background

Even if Fraktur is historically considered a continuation of the Gothic Textura, its formal principle is influenced by the Renaissance. The first Fraktur typeface was developed in Central Europe around 1512 in the environment of Maximilian I's imperial chancellories. In 1525, Albrecht Dürer's book *Underweyſung der meſſung …* was printed in the first Fraktur to be fully realised as a text typeface, the Neudörffer-Fraktur.

Originally designed for the Emperor, Fraktur remained the Germans' predominant style for vernacular texts and typeface for books.
It was able to assert itself alongside roman typefaces until 1941.

Attributes

Fraktur is narrow. It is characterised by a combination of broken and curved shapes, with occasionally broken curves. The forked ascenders on 'b', 'h', 'k', and 'l' are characteristic. The sweeping, sometimes wide upper-case letters are typical, just like its narrow lower-case.

→ Sample: Eskapade

Whenever the black fox jumped the squirrel gazed suspiciously.

A large number of Blackletter typefaces created today do not directly reference the group's historical subcategories. These typefaces often formally reference the broken stroke pattern without incorporating other characteristic Blackletter features. These Blackletter Variations are predominantly used as Headline typefaces.

a

Notice to readers

This collection presents important historical typefaces alongside significant typefaces of the digital era. All in all, these represent a broad spectrum of styles, concepts, and design features. Many historical typefaces have been redesigned for digital use; therefore, several designers and dates are given for some examples (e.g., Didot, 1784 | 1991). These dates are not binding and may reflect either the year of creation or the year the typeface was published. The foundries mentioned first published the typeface or released their digital versions. The classification of the typefaces is based on their Regular weights, with individual Display variants categorized according to their Text styles.

Abbreviations may precede font names. These usually consist of two letters referring to the respective foundry. Typical abbreviations include FF (FontFont), GT (Grilli Type), ITC (International Typeface Corporation), LL (Lineto), LT (Linotype), and MT (Monotype). This guide lists font names in alphabetical order without abbreviations to make the fonts easier to find. Throughout the text, font names are used indiscriminately in both forms, i.e., with and without abbreviations. In practice, you will often find additional abbreviations in font names. These provide information about the font width, weight, application sizes, and the writing systems.

/ 100

Fonts A → Z

List
of Typefaces

Serif

Arnhem, 2002
Athelas, 2008
Baskerville, 1757 | 1978
Beirut Display, 2014
Beirut Text, 2014
Bely, 2016
Bely Display, 2016
Bembo, 1495 | 1929
Beowolf, 1990
Bodoni, 1790 | 1994
Caslon, 1725 | 1990
Didot, 1784 | 1991
Didot Elder, 2004
Dolly, 2001
Fedra Serif, 2003
Filosofia, 1996
Garamond, 1538 | 1989
Georgia, 1996
IBM Plex Serif, 2017
Jenson, 1470 | 1996
Karloff Positive, 2012
Minion, 1989
Mrs Eaves, 1996

Noe Display, 2013
Noe Text, 2015
Pensum, 2016
Rotis Serif, 1988
Sabon, 1964
SangBleu Empire, 2017
Scala, 1991
Sectra, 2013
Spectral, 2017
Swift, 1987 | 2009
Times New Roman, 1931

Slab Serif

Adelle, 2009
American
Typewriter, 1974
Caecilia, 1991
Clarendon, 1845 | 1951
Courier, 1955
Karloff Negative, 2012
Karloff Neutral, 2012
Nordvest, 2016
Rockwell, 1934
Thesis Serif, 1994
Tisa, 2008

Sans Serif

Akkurat, 2004
Akzidenz Grotesk, 1898 | 1958
Antique Olive, 1962
Avant Garde, 1970
Avenir, 1988
Bell Centennial, 1976
Brown, 2011
Cargo, 2003
Circular, 2013
Clan, 2006–2008
Darby Sans Poster, 2014
DIN, 1931 | 1995
Favorit, 2016
Fedra Sans, 2001
Franklin Gothic, 1902 | 1980
Frutiger, 1975 | 2000
Futura, 1927 | 2013
Gill Sans, 1927
Gotham, 2000
Greta Sans, 2012
Gräbenbach, 2016
Haptik, 2014
Helvetica, 1957
IBM Plex Mono, 2017
IBM Plex Sans, 2017
Infini, 2015
International, 2014
Interstate, 1993
Letter Gothic, 1962 | 1989

Meta, 1991
National, 2007
News Gothic, 1908
Nitti, 2008
Noto Sans, 2013
Optima, 1958
Ping, 2019
Replica, 2008
Rotis Sans Serif, 1988
SangBleu Sunrise, 2017
Scala Sans, 1994
Simple, 2002
Syntax, 1969 | 2000
Thesis Sans, 1994
Tisa Sans, 2008
Univers, 1957
Verdana, 1996

Display

Amelia, 1966
Architype Stedelijk, 1968 | 1997
Bauhaus, 1925 | 1975
Blur, 1991
Clifton, 2014–2017
Cooper Black, 1922
Dot Matrix, 1991–1998
FE-Mittelschrift, 1980 | 1997
Kada, 2002
Lo-Res, 1985 | 2001

Lÿno Jean, 2010
Minérale, 2018
Minuscule, 2005
New Alphabet, 1967 | 1997
Orientation, 2018
Pareto, 2016
Template Gothic, 1991
ThreeSix, 2011
Trajan, (113) | 1989

Handwritten

Bello Script, 2004
Brush Script, 1942
Comic Sans, 1995
Mistral, 1953
Zapf Chancery, 1979

Blackletter

Alte Schwabacher,
1470 | 1992
Brokenscript, 1991
Eskapade Fraktur, 2012
Fakir, 2006
Fette Fraktur, 1873 | 1993
Harbour, 1998
Lucida Blackletter, 1991
Old English, 1901 | 2001
San Marco, 1991
Unger Fraktur, 1793 | 2010

Fonts A → Z

Whenever the black fox jumped the squirrel gazed suspiciously.

Name	**Adelle**
Design	Veronika Burian, José Scaglione
Foundry	TypeTogether
Year	2009
Category	(Dynamic) Slab Serif

The type designers José Scaglione and Veronika Burian created Adelle in 2009. They then published it through their foundry TypeTogether.

Adelle's design is characterised by being easy to read and lending a robust pattern to texts. That is caused by the typeface's slab serifs, low contrast and a relatively tall x-height. In addition to its functionality, the details of Adelle's letterforms reveal an independent, dynamic character.

Adelle is particularly suited for use in editorial design. Aside from its being a well-developed typeface for reading long passages of text, the family's fonts have also been optimised for on-screen use.

Whenever the black fox jumped the squirrel gazed suspiciously.

Name	**Akkurat**
Design	Laurenz Brunner
Foundry	Lineto
Year	2004
Category	(Static) Sans Serif

LL Akkurat was made by the Swiss graphic designer and type designer Laurenz Brunner for the foundry Lineto, who first published it in 2004. He produced his first drafts for the typeface while studying at Central Saint Martins in London.

Brunner designed Akkurat as a reaction to the many expressive typefaces from the early 2000s. Akkurat's forms combine the clarity of Swiss typography from the second half of the 20th century (like Helvetica) with the charm of older Sans Serifs (like Akzidenz Grotesk) and translate these into a contemporary style.

Despite its rational design, Akkurat's design was optimised to make it reliable for use as a text typeface. The lower-case 'l' has an out-stroke to differentiate it from the capital 'I' and its lower-case 'g' is double-storey. In addition to its qualities in body text, Akkurat unfurls its character in headlines. Akkurat has been regularly expanded since it was initially published and is extremely popular.

Alice

Whenever the black fox jumped the squirrel gazed suspiciously.

Name	Akzidenz Grotesk
Design	Berthold Design Studio (1898), Günter Gerhard Lange (1958)
Foundry	Berthold	Linotype (Monotype)
Year	1898	1958
Category	(Static) Sans Serif

Akzidenz Grotesk was first published in 1898 by the German foundry H. Berthold AG. In the years leading up to the First World War, the foundry expanded the typeface into a family. Much later – beginning in the 1950s – Günter Gerhard Lange added even more styles. When H. Berthold AG transitioned to photo-typesetting after that, he thoroughly revised Akzidenz Grotesk, making its various styles work more coherently together. Lange was also involved in making the digital versions of Akzidenz Grotesk.

At the beginning of the 20th century, Akzidenz Grotesk was primarily used for so-called 'jobbing printing' (i.e., for advertisements, flyers and posters). The German word for that kind of printing was 'Akzidenzen', and that is how Akzidenz Grotesk received its name. The typeface's clear and reduced forms – as well as its short descenders and ascenders – set it apart from its contemporaries and helped it become one of the first Sans Serif typefaces used for body text.

Those characteristics led to the typeface's great popularity within the New Typography of the 1920s and they especially led to its being used as part of Swiss Typography in the 1950s and 1960s. Indeed, that popularity in the 1950s and 1960s must have been the reason Günter Gerhard Lange and the H. Berthold AG foundry expanded Akzidenz Grotesk to include even more styles and be more consistent as a family.

Due to its clear, reduced Sans Serif character, Akzidenz Grotesk became one of the most used Sans Serif typefaces of the 20th century. It also served as a model for many other Sans Serif type-faces, including Helvetica and Univers. It is still very popular today. The version shown here is Basic Commercial Roman, an adaptation from Linotype.

Erik

Whenever the black for jumped the squirrel gazed suspiciously.

Name	**Alte Schwabacher**
Design	Johann Bämler (1470), URW (1992)
Foundry	Bämler	URW Elsner+Flake
Year	1470	1992
Category	Blackletter (Bastarda)

Schwabacher-style typefaces first appeared in German printing around 1470. Revivals of early Schwabacher typefaces began to be produced in the 19th century. A digital 'Alte Schwabacher' was produced by the German foundry URW in 1992.

Alte Schwabacher is an archetype for a whole blackletter subcategory: Bastarda. These typefaces owe their fame and popularity primarily to their use in the printing of Luther's Bible translations after 1522 (i.e., the Wittenberger Bastarda).

In contrast to its predecessor, the Textura, Bastarda letters have a more accessible, fluid and handwritten nature. They have forms that run wide, which are partly round and partly angular.

Distinguishing features of the Alte Schwabacher typeface include an 'o' that is still round, a 'g' that has a strong horizontal stroke at its top, the characteristically closed capital 'S', and the unusual 'H'. The counters inside its letterforms are the brightest and widest of all typefaces within the Blackletter category.

Bastardas achieved their historical relevance primarily through the Luther Bible and other printed items from the Reformation associated with it. Although Fraktur types replaced the Bastarda style for book typography in German-speaking Europe during the 16th century, Bastardas still retained relevance as secondary typefaces and were used for emphasising words within texts otherwise set in Fraktur. Thanks to its friendly character, Alte Schwabacher is particularly suitable for use in headlines and other display applications.

Whenxever the black fox jumped the squirrel gazed suspiciously.

Name	Amelia
Design	Stanley Davis
Foundry	Visual Graphics Corporation
Year	1966
Category	Display

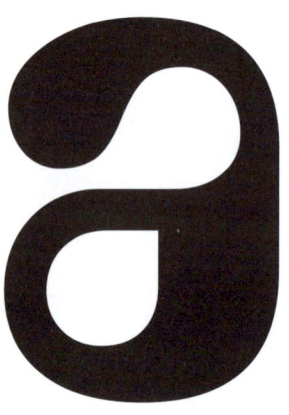

Stanley Davis drew Amelia as an entry to a type-design competition organised by the Visual Graphics Corporation in 1966. The typeface was then published for use in photo-typesetting.

As a product of its time, Amelia's special futuristic shapes encapsulate the hopeful, space-enthusiastic mood of the 1960s. The many teardrop-shaped forms found both as counters inside its letters and on the letters' outer contours are particularly striking.

On the one hand, Amelia's forms are inspired by the technical-looking typefaces used in the 1950s to make checks and other documents machine-readable with the help of the Magnetic Ink Character Recognition (MICR) technology. On the other hand, the typeface was inspired by the psychedelic design language of the 1960s.

With its futuristic, flowing forms, Amelia falls right between hippie culture and space euphoria and was particularly popular during the 1960s.

Martin

Whenever the black fox jumped the squirrel gazed suspiciously.

Name	American Typewriter
Design	Joel Kaden, Tony Stan
Foundry	ITC
Year	1974
Category	(Static) Slab Serif

ITC American Typewriter was designed by Joel Kadan and Tony Stan for the New York-based type design house 'International Typeface Corporation' (ITC) in 1974.

The letterforms of the typeface are based on those from traditional typewriter typefaces used during the 19th and 20th centuries. From a technical point of view, all characters on most typewriters had to occupy the same amount of space – this is the defining feature behind the construction system of 'monospaced' (or fixed-width) typefaces.

American Typewriter was designed as an idealised version of these typewriter typefaces and it emphasises their characteristic texture.

American Typewriter thus simulates typewritten text in print, with the same gentle outer contours, concave serifs and ball terminals famous from typewriter letterforms.

In contrast to the historical models, American Typewriter is not monospaced. Its letters are proportionally spaced, which is why it runs much more evenly and is easier to read than text from a real typewriter. Because of its strong character, the typeface is more suitable for use in headlines and other display applications than for body text.

Whenever the black fox jumped the squirrel gazed suspiciously.

Name	Antique Olive
Design	Roger Excoffon
Foundry	Fonderie Olive
Year	1962
Category	(Dynamic) Sans Serif

Antique Olive was designed by the French typographer Roger Excoffon and published by the Fonderie Olive in 1962. Originally published in 1958 in just an Ultra-Black style with the name 'Nord', the typeface later has more styles added to it and was renamed. Antique Olive became particularly well-known for its use in the Air France logo.

The special shapes in Antique Olive were based on Excoffon's desire to create a new and objective typeface that was not a revival or adaptation of historical forms but a product of science and research. His goal was to use various studies to design a functional Sans Serif that would be optimised for readability.

The most characteristic feature of Antique Olive is its reverse contrast: the letters' horizontal strokes are more emphasised than their verticals, which benefits the eye's movement along a line of text and improves the reading flow, too. The typeface's x-height is very tall and its ascenders and descenders are very short. Antique Olive's letters are open and have vertical terminals ('c', 'e', 's') so that they can transition to each other better. All these features are intended to improve the typeface's legibility in body text.

With its unusual forms, Antique Olive is not only easy to ready but also has a strong character. Even with so much personality, the typeface was unable to prevail outside of France. It undersold against competitors like Helvetica and Univers, which had appeared five years earlier.

Simon

whenever the black fox jumped the squirrel gazed suspiciously.

Name	Architype Stedelijk
Design	Wim Crouwel (1968), David Quay, Freda Sack (1997)
Foundry	The Foundry (Monotype)
Year	1968	1997
Category	Display

Architype Stedelijk is based on poster lettering created by the Dutch graphic designer Wim Crouwel in 1968 as part of his work for the Stedelijk Museum in Amsterdam. In 1997, Crouwel's letterforms were expanded into a complete typeface and published by the London type design studio The Foundry, who was collaborating with Crouwel at that time.

The typeface was developed from lettering Wim Crouwel created for the poster of the design exhibition 'Vormgevers'. The letters are special because they are based on the underlying grid used to design the poster; they make an invisible tool visible in a new way.

Crouwel's letters were constructed on a square grid with an x-height of 5 units, plus units for ascenders and descenders. The stroke endings of the individual modules are rounded off by slight curves. Diagonal connections are created by organic-looking bridges between the modules. This rational, constructed approach gives Architype Stedelijk a technical nature and reduced character.

Although the Architype Stedelijk typeface conveys a digital aesthetic through its pixel shapes, Crouwel's original 1968 design had been created with analogue tools (a pen and ruler) before the first pixel-based screen fonts had even appeared. With his ground-breaking work, Crouwel anticipated the pixel trend of the 1990s.

Whenever the black fox jumped the squirrel gazed suspiciously.

Name	**Arnhem**
Design	Fred Smeijers
Foundry	TypeBy
Year	2002
Category	(Dynamic) Serif

Created by the Dutch type designer Fred Smeijers, Arnhem was originally published by the OurType foundry in 2002. Since 2018, Smeijers' foundry TypeBy has distributed the typeface.

The Arnhem typeface was conceived for the *Nederlandse Staatscourant* daily newspaper as part of a project at the Werkplaats Typografie in Arnhem. Smeijers carried out legibility studies on various versions of its characters to optimise Arnhem as a typeface for newspapers.

The decisive factors for this optimisation were making the x-height very tall and giving Arnhem's letters wide, open counters. These features significantly contribute to legibility. The small gaps between the stems and the diagonals – seen in the letter 'K', for instance – are another special feature. Arnhem has a relatively high stroke contrast, which together with the robust serifs make it the kind of very solid typeface typically used in newspapers. In addition to a 'Normal' style, Arnhem has four other weights. These have been designed so that a text's line-lengths and line-breaks will not change when users switch between one weight and another.

In addition to its special properties relevant for newspaper typesetting, Arnhem has a modern and independent character. The typeface is also particularly suitable for use in book and magazine design.

Whenever the black fox jumped the squirrel gazed suspiciously.

Name	**Athelas**
Design	Veronika Burian, José Scaglione
Foundry	TypeTogether
Year	2008
Category	(Dynamic) Serif

Created by the type designers José Scaglione and Veronika Burian, Athelas was published through their TypeTogether foundry in 2008.

Stylistically, Athelas is based on classic British book types. Its forms were designed so that the typeface achieves the best possible degree of legibility; therefore, they look rather reserved.

Athelas' letterforms have sweeping and elegant curves that do not feature any sharp corners or edges. The letters' counters are opened wide, creating an open and inviting character that facilitates legibility and the formation of syllable and word images. The serifs are subtly bracketed and reminiscent of the calligraphic origins behind all roman typefaces.

Athelas is suitable for use both in book design and in screen-based applications that should have a special book-like character.

Fred

Whenever the black fox jumped the squirrel gazed suspiciously.

Name	**Avant Garde**
Design	Herb Lubalin, Tom Carnase
Foundry	ITC
Year	1970
Category	(Geometric) Sans Serif

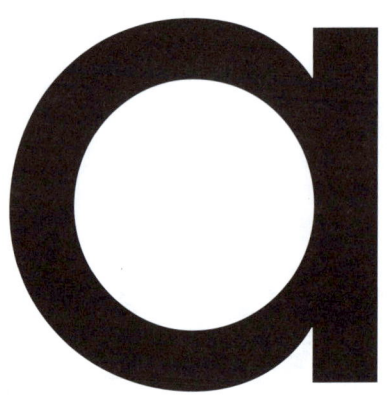

ITC Avant Garde Gothic was created in 1970 by the American type designer Herb Lubalin for the International Typeface Corporation (ITC), a company that he had co-founded.

The basis for the Avant Garde Gothic typeface was a piece of lettering that Lubalin had developed in the late 1960s for the art magazine *Avant Garde*. Later, this was developed into a typeface with Tom Carnase. Lubalin used all the possibilities of the new photo-typesetting technology, including obliquing letters, overlaying letters, and kerning letters – even so much as to place one letterform inside of another. Because of this, Avant Garde Gothic has a large set of upper-case ligatures, where letters are visually connected, or sloped against one another.

Formally, Avant Garde Gothic is based on Geometric Sans Serif typefaces from the 1920s, but it appears even more strictly geometric than they did. For instance, it has no stroke contrast and letterforms like 'a', 'c', and 'o' appear almost circular. The x-height is very tall, leading to the ascenders and descenders being rather short.

Due to its strictly geometric character and its extensive set of upper-case ligatures, Avant Garde Gothic is ideal for use in expressive headlines. The typeface is considered an icon of 1970s-era photo-typesetting and graphic design

Whenever the black fox jumped the squirrel gazed suspiciously.

Name	Avenir
Design	Adrian Frutiger
Foundry	Linotype (Monotype)
Year	1988
Category	(Geometric) Sans Serif

Avenir comes from the Swiss type designer Adrian Frutiger, who created it for the Linotype company in 1988.

Frutiger's motivation in the design of Avenir was to develop a contemporary Geometric Sans Serif. However, it was not to be a simple reissue of a classic example from the 1920s, but a legible design that would be more versatile. The name of his typeface – 'Avenir' is the French word for future – is a reference to Paul Renner's 1927 Futura.

Aside from Futura, Avenir also takes design cues from lesser-known 1920s typefaces, including Neuzeit Grotesk. Avenir's forms may be geometric, but they borrow several features from Humanistic typefaces, including the double-storey lower-case 'a', the out-stroke at the bottom of the 't', slight adjustments to the stroke thickness, and generally wide counter openings. These features ensure that the typeface is very legible, even in smaller type sizes.

Avenir is a hybrid of Geometric and Dynamic Sans Serif typefaces. With its geometric character on the one hand and its Humanistic ties on the other, it is well suited for use in headlines as well as information-heavy applications like signage systems. To a certain extent, Avenir can also be used in body text.

Whenever the black fox jumped the squirrel gazed suspiciously.

Name	**Baskerville**
Design	John Baskerville (1757), Matthew Carter, John Quaranda (1978)
Foundry	Baskerville	ITC
Year	1757	1978
Category	(Transitional) Serif

The term 'Baskerville' refers to types designed by the British typographer and printer John Baskerville around 1757. The ITC New Baskerville typeface is one of many revivals of John Baskerville's designs. It was developed by Matthew Carter and John Quaranda for the International Typeface Corporation, who published it in 1978.

The design of John Baskerville's 18th-century types was made possible because of improvements he had also pioneered in paper-making and other printing processes. The types' design was also influenced by Baskerville's lifelong interest in calligraphy; indeed, when he was younger, he had worked as a writing master.

Baskerville's types are characterised by their relatively strong amount of contrast and their thinner, sharper serifs. The contrast axis in their round letters was more upright than in the other Dynamic Serif typefaces used in John Baskerville's day. His types heralded the movement from Dynamic Serif to Static Serif styles, which is why they are often classified as Transitional Serif typefaces.

Other special features of Baskerville's types include an upper-case 'C' with serifs on both arms, an open loop on the bottom of the lower-case 'g', and a curved tail of the upper-case 'Q'. The italic types include many characters whose decorative elements are inspired by calligraphy.

As a forerunner of the so-called 'modern' typefaces (like Bodoni and Didot), Baskerville had enormous historical significance for 18th-century type design. It was and still is widely used as a book typeface.

Whenever the black fox jumped the squirrel gazed suspiciously.

Name	**Bauhaus**
Design	Herbert Bayer (1925), Edward Benguiat, Victor Caruso (1975)
Foundry	ITC
Year	1925	1975
Category	Display

ITC Bauhaus was created by the type designers
Edward Benguiat and Victor Caruso for the
International Typeface Corporation in 1975. Their
typeface is based on the Universal alphabet,
which itself had been designed in 1925 by Herbert
Bayer, an Austrian typographer who then taught
at the Bauhaus.

Bayer's Universal was commissioned to serve as part
of the identity of the new Bauhaus in Dessau.
An essential part of its design was the attempt to
reduce letters to their purest geometric forms,
removing all the supposedly-decorative elements,
like serifs or stroke contrast. According to the
writing methods then practised at the Bauhaus, the
original version of Universal did not include a set
of capital letters.

Based on Universal's forms, ITC Bauhaus is more
of a reinterpretation than a reissue. For instance,
Benguiat and Caruso designed a set of capital letters
and changed many of Universal's letterforms, too.
They made the round letters geometrically
circular, and the counters of the letters are always
open between the stem and the ends of the strokes
in ITC Bauhaus as well.

With its strictly geometric forms and its expressive
character, ITC Bauhaus is particularly suitable
for use in headlines and other large-format applications.

Whenever the black fox jumped the squirrel gazed suspiciously.

Name	Beirut Display
Design	Luzi Gantenbein
Foundry	Luzi Type
Year	2014
Category	(Dynamic) Serif

Beirut Display was created by the Swiss type designer Luzi Gantenbein for his Luzi Type foundry in 2014.

In comparison with Beirut Text, Beirut Display has a much stronger degree of contrast between its letters' stems and hairlines. The Beirut typefaces' wedge-shaped serifs, as well as their contrast axis, are inspired by handwriting. Yet this particular strand of inspiration is emphasised more in the display variant. Thanks to its strong contrast and wedge-shaped serifs, Beirut Display is particularly suitable for use in expressive headlines and other large-format display applications. It may be supplemented with the Beirut Text typeface.

Whenever the black fox jumped the squirrel gazed suspiciously.

Name	**Beirut Text**
Design	Luzi Gantenbein
Foundry	Luzi Type
Year	2014
Category	(Dynamic) Serif

Beirut Text was created by the Swiss type designer Luzi Gantenbein for his Luzi Type foundry in 2014.

Beirut Text is particularly characterised by its strongly-emphasised wedge-shaped serifs, which are especially evident in the lower-case 'a' and the capital 'S'. In addition to having strong serifs, the typeface is influenced by the nature of hand-writing itself, and that creates a dynamic contrast within its letterforms. Beirut Text is optimised for small reading sizes and is suitable for use in body text. It is complemented by the Beirut Display typeface.

Whenever the black fox jumped the squirrel gazed suspiciously.

Name	**Bell Centennial**
Design	Matthew Carter
Foundry	Linotype (Monotype)
Year	1976
Category	(Dynamic) Sans Serif

Bell Centennial was designed by the British type designer Matthew Carter at Linotype in 1976. Linotype and Carter had been commissioned to deliver a new typeface to AT&T.

To mark its 100th anniversary, the American telecommunications company AT&T commissioned Linotype to create a typeface for use in its telephone books. Their starting point was the Bell Gothic typeface, which Linotype's Chauncey H. Griffith had originally designed back in 1937 for use in New York's telephone books. The typeface's characteristic properties result from the special purpose it was created for.

To accommodate as much content as possible within a small amount of space, Bell Centennial's characters are very narrow. The typeface's letters have a very tall x-height so that readers will be able to quickly and reliably recognise the information printed in telephone books – even with small type sizes like 6pt. The typeface's counters have been made even more open than normal, which offers another significant improvement to legibility. To withstand high-speed printing on thin low-quality paper, Bell Centennial's letters are also equipped with so-called 'ink traps'. These prevent the ink from clogging up the places where strokes intersect. Partially-angular in-strokes and out-strokes on the lower-case letters are also noticeable.

Bell Centennial is an example of typography that, thanks to know-how and the highest level of precision, explored and overcame the technical limitations of its time.

Robert

Whenever the black fox jumped the squirrel gazed suspiciously.

Name	Bello Script
Design	Akiem Helmling, Bas Jacobs, Sami Kortemäki
Foundry	Underware
Year	2004
Category	Handwritten (Script)

A trio of type designers named Akiem Helmling, Bas Jacobs, and Sami Kortemäki made Bello Script in 2004. Together, they form the type designer group Underware, and it was through this foundry that they published Bello Script.

Bello Script draws its inspiration from everyday-variety handwritten signs. The typeface is based on countless hand-made drawings from its three designers, who started by working on the lower-case 'a' and 'e'. They decided to base the design of all remaining characters on those letters since they are the two that are used the most often.

Accordingly, Bello Script has a very handwritten character, but influences from brush calligraphy can also be seen in the capital letters' embellishments. To maintain the impression of real handwriting, Bello Script's letters are precisely aligned. The typeface has more than 60 ligatures, which are both typographical and handwritten in nature. With Bello's 'Caps' style, there is also a set of capitals available that do not have any embellishments.

Bello Script belongs to the comparatively small group of well-produced Handwriting typefaces. It is suitable for use in expressive headlines and other large-format applications.

Whenever the black fox jumped the squirrel gazed suspiciously.

Name	**Bely**
Design	Roxane Gataud
Foundry	TypeTogether
Year	2016
Category	(Dynamic) Serif

Bely comes from the French type designer Roxane Gataud. It was published by the TypeTogether foundry in 2016. Gataud had already begun working on Bely in 2012, while she was studying at the École Supérieure d'Art et de Design Amiens. She later completed it with the help of a TypeTogether scholarship that was intended to help bring the typeface to market.

Above all, Bely is distinguished by the interplay between its strong character and high functionality. The flat serifs at the bottoms of the letters ensure that the typeface's baseline is calm. The letters' open counters help make the typeface very legible, too. At the same time, wedge-shaped serifs on the upper parts of the letters – as well as oversized ascenders and special details like the pointed tail on the capital 'Q' – give Bely much of its personality.

Thanks to its fusion of functionality and character, Bely is well-suited for use in body text and other long texts intended for immersive reading needing a contemporary flair.

Whenever the black fox jumped the squirrel gazed suspiciously.

Name	Bely Display
Design	Roxane Gataud
Foundry	TypeTogether
Year	2016
Category	(Dynamic) Serif

Bely Display is based on the Bely family's text styles. Gataud drove their design parameters to the extreme: in contrast to Bely's text styles, Bely Display has a very strong degree of stroke contrast, which – together with a strongly inclined contrast axis – reinforces the character of the typeface.

Whenever the black fox jumped the squirrel gazed suspiciously.

Name	Bembo
Design	Francesco Griffo (1495), Stanley Morison (1929)
Foundry	Aldus Manutius	Monotype
Year	1495	1929
Category	(Dynamic) Serif

Bembo was designed in 1929 by the British typographer and typographic historian Stanley Morison for the Monotype Corporation. It is based on types produced in 1495 by the Italian punchcutter Francesco Griffo.

The inspiration for the Bembo typeface – Griffo's types from 1495 – was originally cut for the Venetian printer Aldus Manutius, who used them to compose a book by Pietro Bembo, the Italian Humanist. Monotype's typeface revival took its name from him.

Griffo's types gained their historical significance primarily because they were one of the first Serif typefaces to deviate from the handwritten ductus of the Humanistic typefaces of the time. This makes them look more cut than written. The serifs are much sharper and more precise. A calligraphic quality is still retained, however, especially in the lower-case letters.

Bembo's ascenders extend above the tops of the typeface's capital letters. Its x-height is very moderate. The high horizontal stroke inside the lower-case 'e' is striking, as is the long arch of the lower-case 'f' and the straight arch that helps make up the lower-case 'r'.

Thanks to its balanced forms, Bembo became of one of the most-common book typefaces of the 20th century. It is ideal for use in body text and small type sizes.

Whenever the black fox jumped the squirrel gazed suspiciously.

Name	**Beowolf**
Design	Erik van Blokland, Just van Rossum
Foundry	FontFont (Monotype)
Year	1990
Category	(Dynamic) Serif

Beowolf was designed by the Dutch type designers Erik van Blokland and Just van Rossum for their foundry LettError in 1989. Then in 1990, the typeface was published by FontFont under the name FF Beowolf.

What is special about Beowolf is that its letterforms were originally generated at random each time they appeared. The basis of Beowolf was a Dynamic Serif typeface, drawn completely out of straight lines. Each time a letter was typed, the positions of the contour's anchor points would be repositioned at random. The glyphs in Beowolf's character set were not fixed; instead, the typeface could be better understood as being in a permanent state of flux. Since its letterforms' appearances were constantly changing, Beowolf was also known as a 'random font'. The fonts were revised by LettError in 2007 because of technological changes to the PostScript system that had been used until then to randomly generate the letters. Since 2007, the letterforms have no longer been generated entirely at random; instead, one of ten character variants is selected via OpenType features. The Beowolf family has five styles, each of which differs in its degree of letter-form distortion.

Beowolf dates from the early days of digital type design. Thanks to its generative approach to random letterforms, Beowolf became a milestone for contemporary practice.

Lara

Whenever the black fox jumped the squirrel gazed suspiciously.

Name	**Blur**
Design	Neville Brody
Foundry	FontFont (Monotype)
Year	1991
Category	Display

Blur was designed by the British graphic designer and type designer Neville Brody in 1991 for the FontFont foundry he had recently cofounded.

Based on the new possibilities offered by Desktop Publishing in the early 1990s, FF Blur questions the limits of typeface design. Blur's basis is a Static Sans Serif – many suspect Akzidenz Grotesk – that was photographically distorted and then vectorised. By changing the focus, three degrees of alienation emerged: Light, Medium and Bold.

With its imprecise forms, Blur is reminiscent of punk-era print design that was reproduced by photocopying an original (or another copy) again and again. Punk contradicted all the typographic principles of readability and systematics by celebrating an aesthetic of imperfection.

Thanks to its conceptual approach and its striking design language, Blur is still relevant today.

Whenever the black fox jumped the squirrel gazed suspiciously.

Name	**Bodoni**
Design	Giambattista Bodoni (1790), Sumner Stone (1994)
Foundry	Bodoni	ITC
Year	1790	1994
Category	(Static) Serif

The design of the Bodoni typeface can be traced back to work by the Italian type designer Giambattista Bodoni from around 1790. Sumner Stone adapted Bodoni's types into the ITC Bodoni typeface, published by the International Typeface Corporation in 1994.

Inspired by the Transitional Serif typefaces that John Baskerville had designed in the mid 18th century, Bodoni began to also move his work away from following a handwritten ductus, favouring a much more systematic method of letterform construction instead. The resulting types have a very high degree of contrast between their stems and hairlines. The contrast axis is almost vertical.

Together with the typefaces of the Frenchman Firmin Didot, Bodoni's work formed the prototype for all later Static Serif typefaces. Bodoni's forms are crisp and precise. The serifs are unbracketed and usually stand orthogonal to the stem. An upright contrast axis and narrow proportions give the typeface a cool, elevated elegance.

While the constructed forms and high stroke contrast give Bodoni a special aesthetic, those features also make the typeface less legible. Bodoni is therefore somewhat unsuitable for body text. However, it is ideal for use in headlines and other large-sized display applications. With numerous adaptations from large early-20th-century typefoundries, Bodoni's legacy became consolidated and it is still a symbol for elegance and beauty today.

Robin

Whenever the black fox jumped the squirrel gazed suspiciously.

Name	**Brokenscript**
Design	Just van Rossum
Foundry	FontFont (Monotype)
Year	1991
Category	Blackletter (Textura)

FF Brokenscript was designed by Just van Rossum in 1991 and published by the then-recently established FontFont foundry.

Brokenscript is a contemporary interpretation of the Blackletter genre, especially the Textura subcategory. In German, the term for Blackletter translates to 'broken scripts' because of the 'breaks' of 'fractures' in strokes that would otherwise be curved. In keeping with this term, Brokenscript is primarily characterised by its almost geometric, strongly 'broken' letterforms.

In contrast to historical models, van Rossum largely dispensed with stroke contrast in Brokenscript's letterforms. The strokes are almost entirely monolinear. Additionally, Rossum discarded the embellishments common in traditional Blackletter, aside from the split in-strokes at the tops of letters like 'b', 'h', 'k', and 'l'. A striking feature of the typeface is the closed, double-storey lower-case 'a'. That letter's form is based on historical models.

In addition to Bold and Condensed styles, the Brokenscript family includes a variant named Brokenscript Rough. This simulates the 'frayed' texture of print made from roughed up letterpress fonts. By combining a traditional style with contemporary details, van Rossum made Brokenscript suitable for use in expressive headlines and other large-format display applications.

Whenever the black fox jumped the squirrel gazed suspiciously.

Name	**Brown**
Design	Aurèle Sack
Foundry	Lineto
Year	2011
Category	(Geometric) Sans Serif

LL Brown was developed by the Swiss graphic designer and type designer Aurèle Sack and published by the Lineto foundry in 2011.

As the inspiration for Brown, Sack mentions the Johnston typeface Edward Johnston designed for the London Underground (c. 1915), as well as Arno Drescher's Super Grotesk typeface (c. 1930). On closer inspection, however, it becomes clear that both typefaces only served as starting points for Sack. Brown is in no way a fusion or adaptation of those two examples.

Above all, Brown is characterised by its mixture of geometric, monolinear forms with Humanistic, friendly-looking details. This is particularly evident in the lower-case letters. The special relationship between straight lines and curves becomes clear there, which contributes significantly to the typeface's character. The horizontal strokes in the capitals are also rather noticeable. These rest clearly above the optical centre of the letters.

The properties of Brown make it suitable for a range of applications. In addition to various weights and italic styles, the family also includes a 'backslanted' variant.

Whenever the black fox jumped the squirrel gazed suspiciously.

Name	**Brush Script**
Design	Robert E. Smith
Foundry	American Type Founders
Year	1942
Category	Handwritten (Script)

Brush Script was designed by the American
type designer Robert E. Smith for the American
Type Founders Co. in 1942.

Brush Script's very handwritten character
– reminiscent of poster-sized brush-style types –
made it extremely popular in the post-war era,
especially in advertising, posters and shop signage.
In the 1960s, however, the International Style
and the Static Sans Serifs that accompanied it largely displaced Brush Script from graphic design.
Yet, as a result of being licensed by Microsoft and
implemented in its software, Brush Script
experienced a renaissance in Desktop Publishing
during the 1990s.

Characteristics of Brush Script are its flowing,
handwritten character and its high degree of stroke
contrast. In Brush Script's capital letters, the
finely-tapered and partly-curved stroke-endings
are reminiscent of brush lettering. That is quite
a striking feature.

Thanks to its lively, informal character and its
availability on home computers, Brush Script is still
particularly popular in Desktop Publishing.

Whenever the black
fox jumped the squirrel
gazed suspiciously.

Name	**Caecilia**
Design	Peter Matthias Noordzij
Foundry	Linotype (Monotype)
Year	1991
Category	(Dynamic) Slab Serif

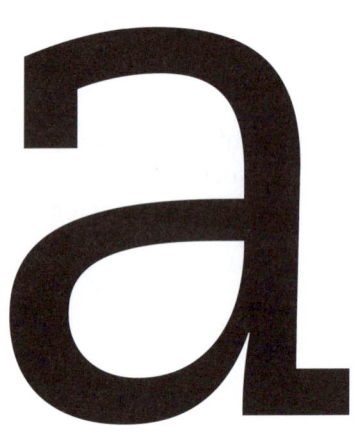

PMN Caecilia was designed by the Dutch type designer Peter Matthias Noordzij and published by Linotype in 1991. The first drafts for Caecilia date back to 1983, when Noordzij was a student at the Royal Academy of Art in The Hague.

The decision to combine a Slab Serif typeface with a Dynamic Principle of Form was conceptually remarkable. Noordzij built his typeface out of Humanistic manuscript styles from the Renaissance, fusing them together with a consistent stroke thickness, giving Caecilia a robust and stable but nevertheless open and friendly character. Its dynamic construction includes wide-open counters and a large x-height, as well as short ascenders and descenders. These all work together to give Caecilia good legibility and a modern character, too.

Thanks to its having successfully combined design approaches that had previously seemed incompatible, Caecilia can be seen as the first Dynamic Slab Serif. Its robust, modern character – together with its readable quality – has made Caecilia very popular.

C

Whenever the black fox jumped the squirrel gazed suspiciously.

Name	Cargo
Design	Gilles Gavillet, David Rust
Foundry	Optimo
Year	2003
Category	(Geometric) Sans Serif

148

Cargo was designed by the Swiss type designers Gilles Gavillet and David Rust in 2002. The Optimo foundry published it in 2003.

Stencil lettering from the Mash stencil-making company served as the inspiration for Cargo's design. The Cargo typeface was originally designed for the visual identity of the Cargo music club at the 2002 Swiss National Exhibition.

Overall, Cargo's letters have narrow proportions. A special feature of their design are the sometimes curved lines (bridges) cut into the letterforms, which lead to Cargo's striking design language.

With its impactful and unusual stencil character, Cargo can be used in many ways, especially for setting expressive headlines and in other large-format display applications.

Adrian

Whenever the black fox jumped the squirrel gazed suspiciously.

Name	**Caslon**
Design	William Caslon (1725), Carol Twombly (1990)
Foundry	Caslon	Adobe
Year	1725	1990
Category	(Dynamic) Serif

The design of the Caslon typeface can be traced back to work by the British punchcutter William Caslon from around 1725. Carol Twombly adapted Caslon's types into the Adobe Caslon typeface, published by Adobe in 1990.

The influence of William Caslon's work on British printing is considerable. Before he began to cut type, there were only a few typefoundries in England. Most fonts had to be imported from abroad, particularly from the Netherlands. The influence of Dutch type design is also visible in Caslon's types.

The Caslon typeface is characterised by an almost vertical contrast axis and compact serifs. Its robust forms give it a warm, inviting character. The strong in-strokes and out-strokes of the lower-case letters are striking, as are the two outward-facing serifs on the capital 'T' and the curved tail on the upper-case 'Q'.

William Caslon's typefaces made England's printing houses independent of imports and they had a lasting influence, particularly in England and America. Caslon was one of the most widely used typefaces for English-language printing into the 19th century and beyond.

Whenever the black fox jumped the squirrel gazed suspiciously.

Name	**Circular**
Design	Laurenz Brunner
Foundry	Lineto
Year	2013
Category	(Geometric) Sans Serif

LL Circular was produced by the Swiss type designer Laurenz Brunner between 2008 and 2013. The Lineto foundry published it in 2013.

The typeface is a contemporary reinterpretation of older examples from the Geometric Sans Serif genre, a category whose most famous representative is Paul Renner's Futura, published in 1927.

Circular's design language consists of a subtle mixture of strict geometry and warm, friendly shapes. In addition to influences from Geometric and Static Sans Serif typefaces, there are also individual Humanistic details that you can find in Circular. What is most striking and characteristic for Circular are the terminals at the ends of the strokes, as well as the typeface's prominent round dots, double-storey lower-case 'a' – atypical in a Geometric Sans Serif – and most particularly, the bracketing between the horizontal stroke and the stem of the lower-case 't'. Thanks to its emphatically contemporary shapes and technical formulation, Circular is suitable for a variety of applications.

Paul

Whenever the black fox jumped the squirrel gazed suspiciously.

Name	**Clan**
Design	Łukasz Dziedzic
Foundry	FontFont (Monotype)
Year	2006–2008
Category	(Dynamic) Sans Serif

The Polish type designer Łukasz Dziedzic developed FF Clan for FontFont between 2006 and 2008.

As a comprehensive typeface family, Clan has 84 type styles. These include seven weights (from Thin through Ultra) and six widths (from Compressed through Extended), as well as corresponding true italics.

Formally, Clan is characterised by its good legibility. Clan's x-height is very tall and its ascenders and descenders are correspondingly short, creating a consistent, calm pattern in text. The counters are wide open. Particularly noticeable are the not quite round, more oval-like curves of the letters. Clan has barely-perceptible stroke contrast. All these features give the typeface an open, friendly character.

With its extensive number of styles, letterforms that are optimised for readability and a dynamic, contemporary character, Clan is suitable for a range of design tasks.

Nina

Whenever the black fox jumped the squirrel gazed suspiciously.

Name	**Clarendon**
Design	Robert Besley, Benjamin Fox (1845), Hermann Eidenbenz (1951)
Foundry	Fann Street Foundry	Haas
Year	1845	1951
Category	(Static) Slab Serif

Clarendon was first designed and cut in 1845 by Robert Besley and Benjamin Fox for the Fann Street Foundry in London. Hermann Eidenbenz adapted it for 20th-century use in 1951 for the Haas Type Foundry.

After Clarendon's resounding success, Besley patented the typeface. Following the end of its three-year protection period, countless competing typefoundries produced copies of Clarendon, which lead to the term 'Clarendon' being applied to a whole category of typefaces. With their heavy eye-catching forms, Clarendon and its copies became a favourite choice to accompany text type-faces in announcements, advertisements, and jobbing printing.

Because of its strongly pronounced serifs, Clarendon is considered a Slab Serif typeface. In contrast to many other Slab Serifs, Clarendon has bracketed transitions between its serifs and stems. Instead of having serifs, some stroke endings are curved, such as the out-strokes on the lower-case 'a' and capital 'R'. Like the strongly pronounced ball terminals on 'a', 'c', 'f', 'g', and 'r', these details appear to be influenced by Static Serif typefaces. Other features of Clarendon include its mild stroke contrast, tall x-height and relatively short ascenders and descenders.

Thanks to its characteristic forms and the striking amount of black it brings onto the page, Clarendon became a very popular typeface. It is still suitable for use as a display typeface and in titling sizes today.

Whenever the squirrel gazed suspiciously.

Name	**Clifton**
Design	Yoann Minet
Foundry	205TF
Year	2014–2017
Category	Display

Clifton was designed by the French type designer Yoann Minet between 2014 and 2017 and published by the 205TF foundry.

Minet sees Clifton as a reinterpretation of a typeface named Athenian, which itself was published in 1896 by the British Type Foundry. Yet compared with its historical reference, Clinton has less pronounced stroke contrast.

Reverse-contrast is Clifton's most prominent feature – the typeface's horizontal strokes are emphasised instead of the verticals. Clifton's letters also have a tall x-height, which Minet added to try to make the design usable as a text typeface. Additionally, the wide, tapering serifs and the teardrop-shaped terminals on letters like the 'a' and the 'r' are striking features.

Characteristic and memorable forms help make Clifton an expressive choice for headline design. The typeface is only limitedly suitable for body text and other passages intended for immersive reading.

Whenever the black fox jumped the squirrel gazed suspiciously.

Name	Comic Sans
Design	Vincent Connare
Foundry	Microsoft
Year	1995
Category	Handwritten (Graphic)

Comic Sans was developed by the American type designer Vincent Connare for Microsoft in 1994 and released with Windows 95.

The motive behind its development came when Connare – then busy helping develop the user interface for 'Microsoft Bob', a software package intended for new PC users – decided to replace Times New Roman with a more appropriate, playful-looking typeface. Connare was inspired by the lettering inside comic book speech bubbles. Accordingly, Comic Sans has a strong handwritten appearance. It is also characterised by asymmetrical, irregular forms and a shaky, uneven baseline.

After Comic Sans was implemented as a system font in Microsoft Windows, its simple and accessible character let to it becoming unprecedentedly popular in Desktop Publishing. While it is viewed mostly with contempt by designers, Comic Sans is otherwise a very popular font for everything that should seem authentic, personal, and informal.

Because of its simple, unpretentious character, Comic Sans became one of the best-known fonts of the 21st century.

Whenever the fox jumped the squirrel gazed suspiciously.

Name	**Cooper Black**
Design	Oswald Bruce Cooper
Foundry	Barnhart Brothers & Spindler
Year	1922
Category	Display

Cooper Black was designed by the American type designer Oswald Bruce Cooper and published by Barnhart Brothers & Spindler in the 1920s.

Because of its extremely excessive stroke thickness, Copper Black is one of the so-called 'fat faces'. Its forms were based on the Cooper Old Style typeface that Cooper had designed three years earlier; that was a Dynamic Serif in the Renaissance style. That typeface's influences and the strong rounding of the letters gives Cooper Black a very warm and friendly character.

Other features of Cooper Black are its tall x-height as well as relatively short ascenders and descenders. Among other things, the narrow lower-case 'f'

– with its characteristic arch – and the sweeping tail of the 'Q' are striking. The counters of the 'o', 'O', and 'Q' are tilted to the left, in contrast to the typeface's otherwise vertical contrast axis. In addition to the upright version, there is also a true italic style.

Cooper Black's round, friendly forms quickly made the typeface a favourite for headlines and other display selections during the 20th century.

The quick brown
fox jumps over the
lazy dog.

Name	**Courier**
Design	Howard Kettler
Foundry	IBM
Year	1955
Category	(Geometric) Slab Serif

Courier was designed by Howard Kettler for the American corporation IBM in 1955.

Developed as a monospace typeface for the typewriters IBM mainly produced at that time, Courier's letters all have the same width, for technical reasons. Another feature of Courier is the consistent stroke thickness in its letters. For the typeface to retain legibility, its x-height was made very tall. Courier's ascenders and descenders are short, too, which give the typeface an even, calm texture.

Despite the many technical limitations its design had to navigate, Courier is an easy-to-read typeface. This is part of what made its jump into the digital era possible. Thanks to its strongly reduced nature, Courier takes up hardly any storage space. It became a standard fall-back font for computers. Courier's even-width characters were ideal for working with code and programming.

Because of its serious, business-like character and its technical features, Courier is still very popular today. Although it is less suitable for body text, it can provide for a distinct look in headlines, as well as in corporate and editorial design.

Whenever the black fox jumped the squirrel gazed suspiciously.

Name	**Darby Sans Poster**
Design	Paul Barnes, Dan Milne
Foundry	Commercial Type
Year	2014
Category	(Dynamic) Sans Serif

Darby Sans Poster comes from the type designers Paul Barnes and Dan Milne. They made the typeface for the Commercial Type foundry in 2014.

Born out of the desire to transfer the elegance of Static Serif typefaces like Bodoni and Didot to a Sans Serif, the inspiration for Darby Sans Poster came from high-contrast British Sans Serif lettering produced between the end of the 18th and the beginning of the 19th century. Darby Sans Poster is Sans Serif, but its letterforms have adopted the strong contrast present in the Serif typefaces from that era.

This design is particularly striking, thanks to its strong stroke contrast and its upright contrast axis. As opposed to Static Serif typefaces, Darby Sans Poster's letters have wide open counters.

Since Darby Sans Poster's letterforms have strong contrast between their stems and hairlines, and also have no serifs, the typeface both attracts attention and exudes elegance. It is complemented by a text variant named Darby Sans.

Max

Whenever the black fox jumped the squirrel gazed suspiciously.

Name	Didot
Design	Firmin Didot (1784), Adrian Frutiger (1991)
Foundry	Didot	Linotype (Monotype)
Year	1784	1991
Category	(Static) Serif

The term Didot refers to typefaces cut by the French punchcutter Firmin Didot, beginning in 1784. The digital revival shown here was designed by Adrian Frutiger for Linotype in 1991.

Firmin Didot came from a family of punchcutters and printers. They were steeped in tradition. During the 18th century, they even worked for the king. Around that time, technological developments were making it possible to produce smoother, better paper. The quality of this new paper allowed for finer letterforms to be printed.

Inspired by earlier progressive developments, including the types from John Baskerville, Firmin Didot pushed letterform rationalisation even further and in the process, he created the proto-types for high-contrast Static Serif typefaces (the types that Giambattista Bodoni cut in this genre were published just a bit later). Didot's type designs opened up a completely new typographic style and were groundbreaking in terms of further development.

Upright contrast axes and strongly-emphasised stroke contrast are characteristic for Didot typefaces. Their hairlines are particularly fine, their serifs are flat and they attach themselves to the letterforms' sturdy stems at right angles, without bracketing.

Because of their clarity and elegance, Didot typefaces are often used for graphics in the cultural and fashion sectors. With their fine details and static letterforms, they are only suitable for body text to a limited extent, but they shine all the more brightly in large type sizes.

Herb

Whenever the black fox jumped the squirrel gazed suspiciously.

Name	**Didot Elder**
Design	François Rappo
Foundry	Optimo
Year	2004
Category	(Static) Serif

Didot Elder comes from the Swiss type designer
François Rappo, who made it in 2004. It is based
on types that the French type designer and printer
duo Firmin and Pierre Didot published in 1819.

Didot Elder has all the characteristic features
of Didot types: a strong emphasis on the verticals,
an upright contrast axis and extreme contrast
between the letters' strong stems and wafer-thin
hairlines. In most cases, the serifs in Didot Elder's
letters attach to the stems at right angles without
any bracketing – also like older Didot types.

What is particularly striking, and where Didot
Elder deviates from earlier Didot revivals, is in the
pointed arrow-like serifs on the capital 'C', 'G',
and 'S'. The lower-case 'y' and 'g' also have unusual
constructions: the descender of the 'y' stretches
downwards vertically, while the descender of the
'g' has an unusual curve.

Didot Elder has all the qualities common to the
Didot genre. It infuses these with a more contemporary appearance and extravagant details.

Whenever the black fox jumped the squirrel gazed suspiciously.

Name	DIN
Design	DIN (1931), Albert-Jan Pool (1995)
Foundry	Berthold	FontFont (Monotype)
Year	1931	1995
Category	(Geometric) Sans Serif

The DIN typeface's origins date back to a design made for the 'Royal Prussian Railway' in c. 1905. Under the direction of the engineer Ludwig Goller, those letterforms were later revised by the Deutschen Institut für Normung and published as the standard DIN-1451 typeface in 1931 for use in the areas of technology and transit. The letters are most well-known for their use on German traffic signs.

The H. Berthold AG foundry published the DIN-Mittelschrift and DIN-Engschrift versions of the typeface in 1981. A digital redesign of DIN named FF DIN was created by the Dutch type designer Albert-Jan Pool for the FontFont foundry in 1995.

Similar to other Geometric Sans Serif typefaces, DIN was originally drawn on a grid with a ruler and compass. This was less due to ideological or aesthetic reasons than for the desire that the lettering could thus be reproducible with any possible tools. When Pool created FF DIN in 1995, he made some changes to the DIN system, including correcting the optical appearance of the letterforms' stroke thicknesses, but he tried to remain true to the character of the original design.

What is striking in DIN is its very geometric, narrow letterforms, whose lower-case letters' terminals end in the direction of the stroke and which have a relatively tall x-height.

DIN's geometric forms give it a serious, precise character. It is still very a popular typeface for a range of applications.

Alisa

Whenever the black fox jumped the squirrel gazed suspiciously.

Name	**Dolly**
Design	Akiem Helmling, Bas Jacobs, Sami Kortemäki
Foundry	Underware
Year	2001
Category	(Dynamic) Serif

A trio of type designers named Akiem Helmling,
Bas Jacobs, and Sami Kortemäki made Dolly in
2001. Together, they form the type designer group
Underware, and it was through this foundry that
they published Dolly.

Dolly was designed with book typography in mind.
This means that the features of the typeface
were optimised for particularly good legibility: the
counters of the letters are generously open, the
contrast axis tilts slightly and the stroke contrast
is lightly distinctive to guarantee an optical texture
in texts, even when they are set in small sizes.

Another feature of Dolly is its calligraphically
inspired nature, which is particularly notable
in the letters' strokes and their serifs. The strokes
all have a handwriting-like swing to them and
usually end in organic-feeling, rounded terminals
– these are especially recognisable on the
lower-case 'a', 'f', and 'r'. The serifs are rounded
asymmetrically and also look more organic than
constructed.

All these features give Dolly a warm, friendly
character. Together with the number of styles in the
family, this qualifies it as a suitable typeface for
extended reading. Dolly has enjoyed great popularity since it was first released.

The quick brown fox jumps over the lazy dog.

Name	**Dot Matrix**
Design	Cornel Windlin, Stephan Müller
Foundry	Lineto, FontFont (Monotype)
Year	1991–1998
Category	Display

Dot Matrix was developed by the type designers Cornel Windlin and Stephan Müller for their Swiss foundry Lineto between 1991 and 1998. It was then distributed by FontFont as FF Dot Matrix.

Conceptually, Dot Matrix is based on Windlin and Müller's banal everyday encounters with rudimentary pixel and display typefaces. The conflict between the progress and the limitation of technology – as well as its effects on typography – was interesting for them.

The letters of the Dot Matrix Text style shown here are based on a 5 × 4-matrix, with an x-height that is four-dots tall and a cap-height of five dots. Ascenders and descenders each take up one point of space, too. The use of dots creates interesting letterforms, especially for letters typically made up of diagonal strokes. Narrow letters like 'i' and 'j' were widened by adding serifs.

With its technically-reduced character, Dot Matrix reproduces the typical image of a low-fidelity typeface used on displays. These qualities make it particularly suitable for headlines and other large-format applications.

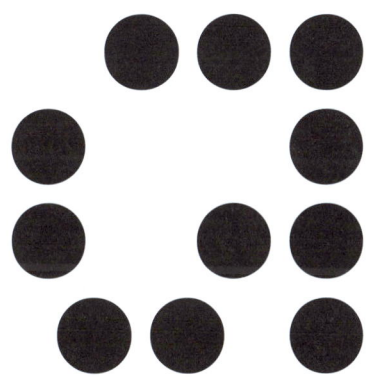

Whenever the black fox jumped the squirrel gazed suspiciously.

Name	**Eskapade Fraktur**
Design	Alisa Nowak
Foundry	TypeTogether
Year	2012
Category	Blackletter (Variations)

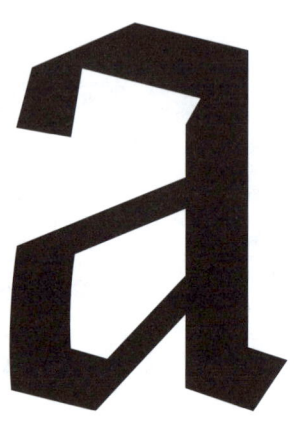

Eskapade Fraktur was designed by the German type designer Alisa Nowak in 2012.

Nowak conceived Eskapade as a superfamily during her studies at the École Supérieure d'Art et de Design Amiens. The basis for the formal language she used came from her research into the historical forms of German writing and printing (especially Blackletter styles).

Characteristic for Eskapade Fraktur are its relatively narrow proportions and the 'broken' strokes of the letterforms. Other features include large ink-traps – especially in the heavier weights – and the subtle incorporation of round forms into the angular pattern of the typeface's design. Eskapade Fraktur's italic styles are based on Sütterlin, a looped German handwriting style from the first half of the 20th century.

The typeface is supplemented within the super-family by Eskapade Roman, a Dynamic Serif based on Humanistic models that can accompany the strong forms of Eskapade Fraktur in body text.

Whenever the fox jumped the squirrel gazed suspiciously.

Name	Fakir
Design	Akiem Helmling, Bas Jacobs, Sami Kortemäki
Foundry	Underware
Year	2006
Category	Blackletter (Variations)

Fakir was made by a trio of type designers named Akiem Helmling, Bas Jacobs, and Sami Kortemäki. Together, they form the type designer group Underware, and it was through this foundry that they published Fakir in 2006.

Their design is a contemporary reinterpretation of Blackletter typefaces. Fakir's formal language is based on Textura-style letterforms – the oldest of the Blackletter categories – written with a broad pen.

Although the may 'breaks' in Fakir's characters give it the overall impression of a Blackletter typeface, the letter shapes themselves are strongly based on those from roman type instead. This gives Fakir's text styles a good degree of legibility. The display styles stand out due to their emphasis on the letters' 'broken' strokes and narrower proportions.
The availability of text and display styles in a single Blackletter family is rare, making Fakir a welcome development.

In addition to text and display styles, the Fakir family also has a font of ornaments that are suitable for a variety of applications.

Whenever the black fox jumped the squirrel gazed suspiciously.

Name	**Favorit**
Design	Johannes Breyer, Fabian Harb
Foundry	Dinamo
Year	2016
Category	(Static) Sans Serif

Favorit was designed and published by the Swiss type design studio Dinamo in 2016. Later, an expanded version was published under the name Favorit Pro.

Among Favorit's many styles, Favorit Lining is the most striking because of the built-in underlines beneath its letters. Even descenders and special characters are integrated into Favorit's system of underlines. Various kinds of underlines – as well as alternate glyphs for the integrated characters – are available via OpenType features.

In addition to having different styles and widths (i.e., Std, Lining, Mono, Extended, and Expanded), Favorit has been expanded to support various writing systems (e.g., Greek, Cyrillic, and Hangul).

Nina

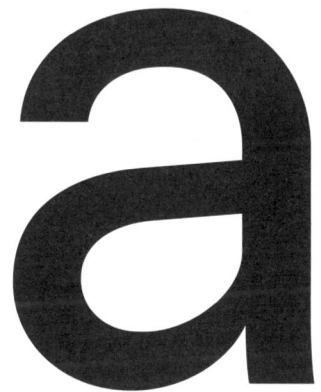

WHENEVER THE FOX JUMPED THE SQUIRREL GAZED SUSPICIOUSLY.

Name	FE-Mittelschrift
Design	Karlgeorg Hoefer (1980), Stephan Müller, Hansjakob Fehr (1997)
Foundry	Dambach-Templin	Lineto
Year	1980	1997
Category	Display

A system of lettering called the 'FE-Schrift' was developed by the German calligrapher and type designer Karlgeorg Hoefer in 1980. This design was adapted in 1997 by Stephan Müller and Hansjakob Fehr for the Swiss foundry Lineto, who published it under the name LL FE-Mittelschrift.

Hoefer designed the lettering system for the West German Ministry of Transportation to prevent license-plate forgery – or at least to make forgery more difficult. Accordingly, the name FE-Schrift stands for 'counterfeit-hindering lettering'.

Each FE-Schrift letter is notable because it is impossible to turn it into another letter by simply adding a stroke, or by taking one away. Normally, this could be done with the letters 'F' and 'E', 'P' and 'R', 'I' and 'L', etc. Hoefer's resulting letterforms look very strange. His lettering system was only put into use several years after its design. Since 2000 it has been the exclusive font used for German license plate lettering.

In 1997, Stephan Müller and Hansjakob Fehr published a digital Version that they expanded to include lower-case letters, punctuation marks, and a condensed variant.

Whenever the black fox jumped the squirrel gazed suspiciously.

Name	Fedra Sans
Design	Peter Biľak
Foundry	Typotheque
Year	2001
Category	(Dynamic) Sans Serif

Fedra Sans was designed in 2001 by the Slovak type designer Peter Biľak and published by the Dutch foundry he established, Typotheque.

Part of the Fedra superfamily, Fedra Sans was initially created during a proposed redesign for a German insurance company's identity that was being undertaken by the Parisian design studio Intégral Ruedi Baur. That redesign was ultimately not implemented, allowing Biľak to expand Fedra Sans into a multi-script superfamily and distribute those fonts himself.

The combination of rational and Humanistic design approaches is a key characteristic of Fedra. While all forms have certain objectivity, rounds and other curves bring an informal, accessible nature to the typeface's texture. Fedra has wide open counters, ensuring for good legibility both on screens and in print. Among other things, the diamond-shaped 'i' dots are also quite characteristic.

The Fedra superfamily has been extensively expanded to support many languages and writing systems. The size of the Fedra superfamily, coupled with its readable and accessible nature, make it well suited for a variety of applications.

Whenever the black fox jumped the squirrel gazed suspiciously.

Name	Fedra Serif
Design	Peter Biľak
Foundry	Typotheque
Year	2003
Category	(Dynamic) Serif

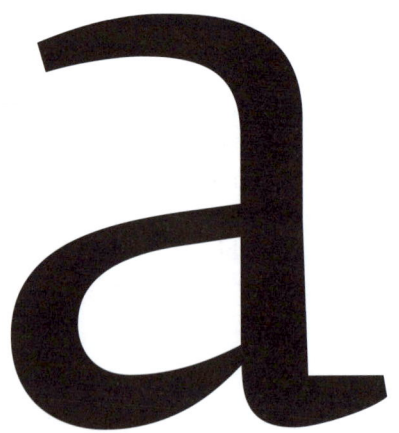

Fedra Serif was designed in 2003 by the Slovak type designer Peter Biľak and published by the Dutch foundry he established, Typotheque.

The typeface is part of the Fedra superfamily, which itself was initially created during a proposed redesign of a German insurance company's identity being undertaken by the Parisian design studio Intégral Ruedi Baur. That redesign was ultimately not implemented, allowing Biľak to further expand Fedra into a multi-script superfamily and distribute the fonts himself.

The combination of rational and Humanistic design approaches is a key characteristic of Fedra. While all forms have certain objectivity, rounds and other curves bring an informal, accessible nature to the typeface's texture. Fedra has wide open counters, ensuring for good legibility both on screens and in print. Among other things, the diamond-shaped 'i' dots are also quite characteristic.

The Fedra superfamily has been extensively expanded to support many languages and writing systems. The size of the Fedra superfamily, coupled with its readable and accessible nature, make it well suited for a variety of applications.

𝕸henever the black fox jumped the squirrel gazed suspiciously.

Name	**Fette Fraktur**
Design	Alexander & Conrad Bauer
Foundry	Bauer	Linotype (Monotype)
Year	1873	1993
Category	Blackletter (Fraktur)

Originally designed by Johann Christian Bauer's sons Alexander and Conrad Bauer, Fette Fraktur was published in 1873 through Bauer's Frankfurt-based typefoundry. Numerous other foundries brought out their own variants of the design, too. The version shown here is Linotype's, from 1993.

A display typeface, Fette Fraktur's characteristics met a need present in the mid 19th century for heavy, striking typefaces that could be used in advertising. It became one of the most commonly-used Blackletter typefaces, and it is available today thanks to the many revivals that have been published.

The typeface is characterised by an extreme degree of stroke contrast. Fette Fraktur's heaviness lies in its thickest strokes being a great many times thicker than its hairlines. Especially in the capital letters, this leads to elegant, intricate shapes. Another characteristic of Fette Fraktur are the thin, pointed stroke endings on both upper-case and lower-case letters, the split ascenders on e.g., the 'b', and 'k', or the curved in-strokes on the 'p', 'v', 'w', and 'y'. The capital 'W' is quite pictorial and very impressive-looking.

Fette Fraktur attracts a lot of attention because of its intricate, pictorial capitals and pointed, high-contrast lower-case letters. During its time, Fette Fraktur fulfilled a display typeface's responsibilities. Even today, it is suitable for use in large sizes, as well as for emphasis.

Whenever the black fox jumped the squirrel gazed suspiciously.

Name	**Filosofia**
Design	Zuzana Licko
Foundry	Emigre
Year	1996
Category	(Static) Serif

Filosofia was designed by the American type designer Zuzana Licko and published by her digital font foundry Emigre in 1996.

Licko created Filosofia as an interpretation of the Static Serif typefaces designed at the end of the 18th century by the Italian typographer Giambattista Bodoni. These are characterised by their rationalised and constructed forms, as well as by their very distinctive stroke contrast. However, those features do not aid legibility, especially in small type sizes.

Based on designs by Giambattista Bodoni, Filosofia represents Licko's attempt to optimise Bodoni's types in terms of legibility and performance in smaller type sizes. Its forms are closely related to Bodoni's, but overall they look more organic and less strict. The contrast between its stems and hairlines is much less pronounced than in other interpretations that have been made of Bodoni's work. Filosofia's serifs are not rationalised in a rectangular manner, but have rounded shapes and thus refer to the real historical print image.

The subtle shapes of Filosofia Regular are joined by those of the more rationally designed Filosofia Grand style, which also includes a unicase version. Filosofia is suitable for body text and allows for new possibilities when it comes to designing head-lines and other display applications.

Whenever the black fox jumped the squirrel gazed suspiciously.

Name	Franklin Gothic
Design	Morris Fuller Benton (1902), Victor Caruso (1980)
Foundry	American Type Founders	ITC
Year	1902	1980
Category	(Transitional) Sans Serif

Franklin Gothic was designed in 1902 by the American type designer Morris Fuller Benton at the American Type Founders Co. foundry. In 1980, Victor Caruso adapted the typeface as ITC Franklin Gothic for the International Typeface Corporation. In 2008, another revision was published; named ITC Franklin, this was produced by David Berlow.

In particular, Benton was inspired during his design process by American wood type, but he was also looking at contemporary European Sans Serif typefaces like Akzidenz Grotesk. Franklin Gothic includes features inspired by many sources, which is part of what distinguishes it as a Transitional Sans Serif (also sometimes called 'American Gothics').

Franklin Gothic has a moderate amount of stroke contrast, which is particularly noticeable in the transitions from curves to stems. As can be seen in the double-storey forms of the 'a' and 'g', Franklin Gothic borrows features from Serif typefaces, which is another design feature of Transitional Sans Serifs. Thanks to its tall x-height, Franklin Gothic is also suitable for setting texts intended for immersive reading.

Franklin Gothic is the archetypal Transitional Sans Serif typeface and is representative of the kind of designs in that genre created in the USA at the beginning of the 20th century. Through its clear forms and moderate contrast, Franklin Gothic is suitable for use in both expressive headlines and body text.

Yoann

Whenever the black fox jumped the squirrel gazed suspiciously.

Name	Frutiger
Design	Adrian Frutiger
Foundry	Stempel	Linotype (Monotype)
Year	1975	2000
Category	(Dynamic) Sans Serif

Frutiger was designed by Adrian Frutiger in 1975. In 2000, Linotype Design Studio revised it in collaboration with Frutiger and re-published it as Frutiger Next.

The Frutiger typeface had its start in 1968 when an early version of the design named Roissy was commissioned for the signage system inside the new Charles de Gaulle airport, which was then under construction in Roissy near Paris. The design was used for the first time in 1975. The 'Frutiger' type-face was published in 1976 as a commercial typeface by the D. Stempel AG foundry in Frankfurt.

Like Adrian Frutiger's earlier Univers typeface, Frutiger is a milestone in the development of Sans

Serif typefaces. To meet the signage system's requirements, Adrian Frutiger started from the neutral-looking Univers and designed his newer typeface to be more legible and have a more noticeable character. To achieve this, he combined the properties of the Sans Serif genre with the Humanistic forms of Dynamic Serif typefaces. Characteristic for Frutiger are its open forms, tall x-height and friendly nature. Through the vertical and horizontal stroke terminals, the horizontal reading flow is emphasised.

Thanks to its dynamic character, Frutiger is highly legible, which makes it particularly suitable for body text and signage systems. Because of this, Frutiger became very widespread, in terms of its use, and is a popular typeface today.

Emilie

Whenever the black fox jumped the squirrel gazed suspiciously.

Name	Futura
Design	Paul Renner (1927), ParaType (2013)
Foundry	Bauer	ParaType
Year	1927	2013
Category	(Geometric) Sans Serif

Futura was designed by the German typographer Paul Renner between 1924 and 1926. The Bauer Type Foundry published it in 1927.

The typeface is considered to be the first and most well-known Geometric Sans Serif. It was designed to create 'the typeface of our time', in the spirit of the 1920s avant-garde. The concept behind the design was to distil letters down to their bare essentials and reduce them to their basic forms. In contrast to the Bauhaus typographers, Renner did not dogmatically design with triangles, circles and squares. Instead, he drew his inspiration primarily from the Ancient Roman Capitalis Monumentalis.

Above all, Futura's chief characteristic is that it has letterforms that seem to be geometric, especially when you look at the lower-case. Another key feature is its seemingly consistent stroke thickness; in fact, letters like the 'o' that seem to be round are slightly elliptical instead. In places where two strokes meet, their thicknesses are adjusted so that they seem optically the same. Futura runs rather wide and does not have a very tall x-height.
Its ascenders extend above the height of the capital letters. Other recognisable features in Futura are the single-storey 'a', the 'j' and 't' that lack round out-strokes, and a circular-looking spurless 'G'. Since the 'c' is often followed by an 'h' in German, the stroke-endings on that letter's right-hand side are concise and vertical.

Thanks to its geometric, clear and reduced forms, Futura has a timeless and elegant character.
This has helped to make it one of the most successful 20th-century typefaces.

Indra

Whenever the black fox jumped the squirrel gazed suspiciously.

Name	**Garamond**
Design	Claude Garamont (1538), Robert Slimbach (1989)
Foundry	Garamont	Adobe
Year	1538	1989
Category	(Dynamic) Serif

Behind the 'Garamond' name are several typefaces cut around 1538 by the French punchcutter Claude Garamont (or Garamond). The version shown here was adapted by Robert Slimbach for Adobe in 1989 as Adobe Garamond.

Today, Claude Garamont can easily be considered one of the most influential type designers in history. With his typefaces, he not only influenced the work of his contemporaries; Garamont's types are some of the most-often adapted designs in history. While original prints of his types served as the basis for the roman styles of Adobe Garamond, the family's italic styles are based on types from Robert Granjon, who was also active during Garamont's time.

Characteristic for Garamond is its open, light and even texture. The letterforms are differentiated and show their handwritten origins. These roots can also be found in the inclined axis and the moderate stroke contrast. The open counters make Garamond easy to read and give the typeface a warm, flowing and organic nature The asymmetrical distribution of the counterforms inside the 'a' and 'e' is striking.

The Humanistic qualities and easy readability in body text brought Claude Garamont's typefaces international attention and led to their being frequently adapted. Slimbach's Adobe Garamond is one of the most authentic interpretations and is ideal for use in book typography and other applications where immersive reading is encouraged.

Whenever the black fox jumped the squirrel gazed suspiciously.

Name	Georgia
Design	Matthew Carter
Foundry	Microsoft
Year	1996
Category	(Dynamic) Serif

Georgia was designed in 1996 by the British type designer Matthew Carter for Microsoft.

The typeface was especially intended for use in small type sizes on computer screens. Carter defined the contours of its letterforms pixel for pixel, comparing renderings of the different sizes with his design. Only then did he covert his glyphs into the typeface's final vector forms. This is the reason for Georgia's excellent appearance on screen, even at low resolutions.

Georgia's design was influenced by the so-called 'Scotch Roman' typefaces, which are classified as Static Serifs. You can see this in Georgia's vertical contrast axis, its flat serifs on the lower-case letters' ascenders, as well as on the horizontal flag of the 'g' and the straight stroke at the top the 't'. However, in contrast to that influence, Georgia's letters also have a moderate degree of stroke contrast, as well as dynamic forms, a tall x-height, and generally open counters – which were primarily added to improve on-screen legibility.

Since Georgia was implemented in both Microsoft's as well as Apple's operating systems, websites could rely on it as a font to use to display their text, allowing for online font selections to be made independent of specific platforms. This contributed to Georgia's popularity significantly.

Whenever the black fox jumped the squirrel gazed suspiciously.

Name	Gill Sans
Design	Eric Gill
Foundry	Monotype
Year	1927
Category	(Dynamic) Sans Serif

Gill Sans was designed by the British sculptor and type designer Eric Gill for Monotype in 1927.

The work was based on a sign that Gill had lettered for a bookshop. Following Stanley Morison's invitation, he developed a complete typeface out of it. Morison and Monotype hoped it could compete with the new Sans Serifs that were coming out of Germany at that time. In particular, however, Gill had been inspired by the letters from the London Underground signage system, which itself had been designed by Edward Johnston. In Gill's younger years, he and Johnston had been close friends and collaborators.

Like Futura, the capital letters in Gill Sans are based on the Ancient Roman Capitalis Monumentalis. The typeface's lower-case letters have skeletons resembling those of Dynamic Serif typefaces from the Renaissance. That legacy is particularly visible in the double-storey 'a' and 'g'. Gill Sans has mild contrast, its counters are wide open, and its x-height is tall. Its ascenders and the tops of the capital letters both reach up to the same height. Vertical stroke-endings – like those on the C, c, S, s and e – are a characteristic feature of the typeface, as is the special shape the horizontal stroke of the 't' takes.

Thanks to its extraordinary mixture of Humanist forms inspired by Dynamic Serif typefaces, coupled with more modern design parameters from the Sans Serif genre, Gill Sans quickly became popular. The typeface is still beloved around the world today.

Martin

Whenever the black fox jumped the squirrel gazed suspiciously.

Name	Gotham
Design	Jonathan Hoefler, Tobias Frere-Jones
Foundry	Hoefler&Co.
Year	2000
Category	(Geometric) Sans Serif

Gotham was designed by Jonathan Hoefler and Tobias Frere-Jones in 2000.

It took its inspiration from a style of early twentieth-century lettering used by draftspersons and often seen on the facades of commercial buildings in New York City. First appearing in the pages of GQ magazine in 2001, Gotham gained international attention in 2008, after Barack Obama's presidential campaign adopted it.

As in its models, Gotham's forms are based on rational and geometric construction. Most of the rounds look almost circular, making Gotham run quite wide. However, Gotham breaks with the strict grid in some details, leading to forms that have Humanistic influences. Therefore, Gotham looks determined, but also friendly and inviting.

One of the most popular typefaces of the 21st century, Gotham is in the permanent collection of the Museum of Modern Art in New York. It is suitable for setting both body text as well as headlines and other large-format display applications.

Whenever the black fox jumped the squirrel gazed suspiciously.

Name	**Gräbenbach**
Design	Wolfgang Schwärzler
Foundry	Camelot
Year	2016
Category	(Static) Sans Serif

Gräbenbach was designed by the German type designer Wolfgang Schwärzler and released in 2016 as part of Camelot Typefaces.

Inspired by early Sans Serif typefaces like Venus and Monotype Grotesque, as well as by Akzidenz Grotesk, Schwärzler supplemented Gräbenbach's letterforms by adding stroke terminals reminiscent of brush lettering.

The skeletons of Gräbenbach's letters are common to other Static Sans Serif typefaces. There is no noticeable stroke contrast in Gräbenbach's letters, and their counters are closed. This gives the typeface a rational character, which is complemented by the unusual terminals at the ends of its strokes.

Those pointed, curved details can best be seen in the lower-case letters. The double-storey 'a' – with its top curve extending far out to the left – is a particularly striking feature of the typeface, as is the curved flag of the 'a' and the pointed terminal of the 'r'.

Gräbenbach's pointed details set it apart from other Sans Serifs and make it a characterful alternative to many contemporary Static Sans Serif typefaces.

Whenever the black fox jumped the squirrel gazed suspiciously.

Name	Greta Sans
Design	Peter Biľak, Nikola Djurek
Foundry	Typotheque
Year	2012
Category	(Dynamic) Sans Serif

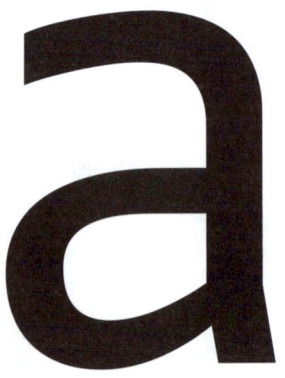

Greta Sans was designed in 2012 by the Slovak type designer Peter Biľak (in collaboration with Nikola Djurek) and published by the Dutch Typotheque foundry.

Biľak conceived Greta as a comprehensive super-family, whose letterforms would be related to each other across all widths and weights. The forms of Greta Sans are influenced by Humanistic type-faces and they are designed for readability. Their x-height is very tall, the letterforms and counters are wide open, and ascenders extend above the tops of capital letters. All this gives Greta a friendly, accessible character.

In addition to having a large number of styles, the Greta superfamily also has Mono, Text, Display and Grande variants available. The fonts support over one hundred languages, as well as multiple writing systems (e.g., Latin, Cyrillic, Greek, Arabic, Hebrew and Thai).

Alisa

Whenever the black fox jumped the squirrel gazed suspiciously.

Name	**Haptik**
Design	Reto Moser, Tobias Rechsteiner
Foundry	Grilli Type
Year	2014
Category	(Geometric) Sans Serif

GT Haptik was developed between 2010 and 2014 by Reto Moser and Tobias Rechsteiner for the Swiss foundry Grilli Type.

The concept behind Haptik's design was to develop a typeface whose upper-case letters and numbers could be recognisable by feeling and which would be readable with closed eyes; this explains Haptik's unusual letterforms. Lower-case letters were then developed so that Haptik could be used as a text typeface, too.

Formally, Haptik is based on a geometric construction principle. Its upper-case letters are monolinear without any optical corrections. Capital letters vary greatly in width, for differentiation reasons. The capital 'C', 'G', and 'R' have special shapes to help guide the fingers as they feel the letterforms. The Rotalic style shown here, which complements the upright and oblique styles, does not simply slant the characters but rotates entire letters by 15°. Intended to be read by touching it blindfolded, a rotalic proofed to be the more suitable solution for a touchable italic style.

With its experimental shapes and rotated glyphs, Haptik Rotalic attracts attention and is suitable for a variety of applications.

The quick brown fox jumps over the lazy dog.

Name	Harbour
Design	Gareth Hague
Foundry	Alias
Year	1998
Category	Blackletter (Variations)

Harbour was designed in 1998 by the British type designer Gareth Hague and published by his Alias foundry.

This contemporary typeface combines roman forms with blackletter elements – with an emphasis being on the more easy-to-read elements of the roman. Harbour has noticeable stroke contrast and a strongly inclined contrast axis. This combination of curved, calligraphic elements and constructed shapes is particularly striking. While the contrast distribution and the 'breaks' in the lowercase letters' strokes are reminiscent of medieval calligraphy, Harbour's serifs and the basic forms of its capitals are borrowed from roman type.

With its mixture of calligraphic Blackletter-style elements and basic roman forms, Harbour represents an interesting reinterpretation of the Blackletter genre.

Whenever the black fox jumped the squirrel gazed suspiciously.

Name	Helvetica
Design	Max Miedinger, Eduard Hoffmann
Foundry	Haas, Stempel	Linotype (Monotype)
Year	1957
Category	(Static) Sans Serif

Helvetica was designed by the Swiss typographer Max Miedinger in collaboration with Eduard Hoffmann for the Haas Type Foundry in 1957.

The design was first published under the name Neue Haas Grotesk. It was intended to expand the Swiss foundry's repertoire to include a Sans Serif typeface that could compete with Akzidenz Grotesk. Even if the two typefaces are similar, Miedinger and Hoffmann endeavoured to improve Akzidenz Grotesk's irregularities while creating Helvetica.

Based on Akzidenz Grotesk, Helvetica is strongly reduced and characterised by its solid texture. Its letterforms are closed and have no visible stroke contrast. They have a tall x-height as well as moderate ascenders and descenders. Strokes end in either horizontal or vertical terminals, which contributes to the typeface's compact and steadfast nature.

The letterforms in Helvetica are very even and thus form a clear and neutral-looking texture. This objectivity led to Helvetica becoming one of the most used typefaces in the world – it is familiar to many people, not just designers. Helvetica has served as a model for many imitations and new interpretations as well.

The quick brown fox jumps over the lazy dog.

Fonts A → Z

218

Name	**IBM Plex Mono**
Design	Mike Abbink, Bold Monday
Foundry	IBM, Bold Monday
Year	2017
Category	(Static) Sans Serif

IBM Plex Mono was designed by the Dutch foundry Bold Monday in cooperation with Mike Abbink for the American company IBM in 2017.

It is part of IBM Plex superfamily, which formally and conceptually refers to the company's logo. Plex Mono is derived from Plex Sans, but it is also inspired by early typewriter typefaces that IBM used to manufacture.

In line with the IBM logo, the curves inside the typeface's letters are angular, while the outer curves are round. This feature can best be seen in the lower-case 'a', 'f', 'g', 'j', 'l', and 't'. Due to all of its characters having been adjusted to have the same width, the lower-case 'f', 'i', 'k', and 't' each have particularly striking forms.

Thanks to its many sources of formal inspiration – which are all subtly balanced out – as well as its typewriter aesthetic, IBM Plex Mono is very suitable for use in headlines and other display applications. The Plex superfamily also has the IBM Plex Sans and IBM Plex Serif typefaces in it.

Fred

Whenever the black fox jumped the squirrel gazed suspiciously.

Name	**IBM Plex Sans**
Design	Mike Abbink, Bold Monday
Foundry	IBM, Bold Monday
Year	2017
Category	(Static) Sans Serif

IBM Plex Sans was designed by the Dutch foundry Bold Monday in cooperation with Mike Abbink for the American company IBM in 2017.

It is part of IBM Plex superfamily, which formally and conceptually refers to the company's logo. Plex Sans draws inspiration from Sans Serif typefaces created during the late 19th and early 20th century (e.g., Akzidenz Grotesk, Franklin Gothic).

IBM Plex Sans has barely visible stroke contrast, which is particularly noticeable in the transitions from the letters' curves to their stems. In line with the IBM logo, the curves inside the letters are angular, while the outer curves are round. This feature can best be seen in the lower-case 'a', 'f', 'g', 'j', 'l', and 't'.

Thanks to its many sources of formal inspiration – which are all subtly balanced out – IBM Plex Sans is a striking Sans Serif that is suitable both for use in text as well as headlines and other display applications. The Plex superfamily also has the IBM Plex Mono and IBM Plex Serif typefaces in it.

Robert

Whenever the black fox jumped the squirrel gazed suspiciously.

Fonts A → Z

Name	**IBM Plex Serif**
Design	Mike Abbink, Bold Monday
Foundry	IBM, Bold Monday
Year	2017
Category	(Static) Serif

IBM Plex Serif was designed by the Dutch foundry Bold Monday in cooperation with Mike Abbink for the American company IBM in 2017.

It is part of IBM Plex superfamily, which formally and conceptually refers to the company's logo. Formally, Plex Serif draws inspiration from from numerous 17th to 19th century models, most notably fonts inspired by Nicholas Kis (Ehrhardt, Janson) and Bodoni. Plex Serif italic references 17th and 18th century Transitional typefaces, whereas Plex Serif roman leans a bit more towards the verticality of Static Serif types such as Bodoni, but also the less rigid Scotch types.

The characters in IBM Plex Serif have moderate stroke contrast and a vertical contrast axis. While the upper serifs on the lower-case letters are wedge-shaped, the bottom serifs are rectangular and attach to the stems without any bracketing. Teardrop-shaped ball terminals are borrowed from neoclassical Static Serif typefaces like Bodoni; these can be found on the lower-case letters like the 'a', 'c', 'f', 'g', and 'r'.

Thanks to its many sources of formal inspiration – which are all subtly balanced out – IBM Plex Serif is suitable for use both as a text typeface as well as in headlines and other display applications. The Plex superfamily also has the IBM Plex Sans and IBM Plex Mono typefaces in it.

Whenever the black fox jumped the squirrel gazed suspiciously.

Name	**Infini**
Design	Sandrine Nugue
Foundry	CNAP
Year	2015
Category	(Dynamic) Sans Serif

Infini was developed by Sandrine Nugue, a French graphic designer and type designer, for the Centre national des arts plastiques (CNAP) in 2015.

The typeface was created as part of the CNAP's 'Graphisme en France' program. A competition initiated by Véronique Marrier aimed to find a typeface design that could later be distributed as freely available fonts to raise awareness about typeface designers' professional roles.

Nugue's concept rests on a connection of lettering history to design practice within one typeface. Infini takes its historical character from the inscriptional lettering of antiquity and mixes it with a contemporary type-design concept. The tapering of its stems, its obliquely-shaped contours and stroke-endings – as well as its open counters – all work together to give the typeface a dynamic impact.

In addition to bold and italic styles, Infini is complemented by its own set of pictograms and a comprehensive number of ligatures. Thanks to its exceptional character, Infini is suitable for both body text and use in large-sized settings like display typography or titles.

Together with an explanatory specimen, the Infini fonts can be downloaded free of charge from the CNAP website: www.cnap.fr

Whenever the black fox jumped the squirrel gazed suspiciously.

Name	International
Design	Stefan Gandl
Foundry	Neubau
Year	2014
Category	(Static) Sans Serif

NB International was designed and published by the Austrian graphic designer Stefan Gandl in 2014 as part of the design for the *Neubau Forst Archive* catalogue.

Founded in 2001, the Berlin design studio Neubau developed a detailed visual archive of Berlin's trees over five years. For this extensive project, Stefan Gandl decided that a suitable typeface was needed; this is how NB International came about.

Based on Static Sans Serif typefaces like Helvetica or Univers, NB International's design is greatly reduced. Gandl created it on a geometric grid. Its letterforms are closed and look even. They have no stroke contrast. Their strokes end in vertical or horizontal terminals. NB International has a tall x-height and relatively short ascenders and descenders, leading to a compact and uniform texture. NB International's capitals are slightly narrower than the geometry of Helvetica; additionally, the typeface is characterised by tiny curves on all the corners. Despite NB International's geometric construction, those corners give the typeface a certain softness.

Whenever the black fox jumped the squirrel gazed suspiciously.

Name	Interstate
Design	Tobias Frere-Jones
Foundry	Font Bureau
Year	1993
Category	(Geometric) Sans Serif

Interstate was developed by the American type designer Tobias Frere-Jones for the Font Bureau foundry in 1993.

The basis for Interstate was the typeface used on American highway signage since the 1940s. Frere-Jones' concept was to transfer the properties that contributed to good legibility at a distance at high speeds to a typeface intended for use in body text, even when it would be set at small type sizes.

Interstate has low stroke contrast and a tall x-height, as well as short ascenders and descenders. Legibility is enhanced by its wide, open counters and by the individual terminal designs of its descenders, which contribute to their distinguishability. The cut-off out-stroke of the lower-case 'g' is characteristic of Interstate, for instance.

Because of its properties, Interstate had proved to be a good typeface for reading. It is also suitable for use in large type sizes.

Lucas

Whenever the black fox jumped the squirrel gazed suspiciously.

Name	**Jenson**
Design	Nicolas Jenson (1470), Robert Slimbach (1996)
Foundry	Jenson	Adobe
Year	1470	1996
Category	(Dynamic) Serif

Behind the 'Jenson' name are types cut around 1469 by the French typographer and punchcutter Nicolas Jenson. At that time, he was active in Venice. The version shown here was adapted by the American type designer Robert Slimbach for Adobe in 1996.

Jenson's types are considered the first to have been printed according to the roman model, whose origins lay in Humanistic manuscripts from the Renaissance. Jenson's types are characterised by their balance and by their dynamic letterforms, which have moderate stroke contrast. The elongated diagonal crossbar of the lower-case 'e' is particularly characteristic of Jenson's roman.

While reviving the typeface, Slimbach referenced to the high-quality books printed by Jenson, since none of Jenson's fonts of metal type have survived. Based on those original prints, Slimbach developed three optical sizes so that Adobe Jenson could be used for typesetting different sizes of text.

Thanks to its balanced forms, Jenson revivals are some of the most-used book typefaces. Adobe Jenson is ideally suited for body text, even in very small text sizes.

THE QUICK BROWN FOX JUMPS OVER THE LAZY DOG.

Name	Kada
Design	Joel Nordstroem
Foundry	Lineto
Year	2002
Category	Display

LL Kada was designed by Joel Nordstroem and published by the Swiss foundry Lineto in 2002.

The inspiration for Kada was the logo of coffee machines made by a company called RAYGIL. The logo's letters were probably based on a rounded Sans Serif typeface named Frankfurter, originally designed by Alan Meeks and Nick Belshaw.

A key feature of Kada is its reduced character. The typeface's letters are all capitals and they have simple geometric construction, paired with rounded stroke endings. Designed in the style of a stencil typeface, Kada has prominent incisions that open up its counters and allow the letterforms to be realised as stencils, too.

With its simple, rounded style, Kada has a friendly and modern look. The typeface is particularly suited for use in titling and other display applications that take large sizes.

Whenever the black fox jumped the squirrel gazed suspiciously.

Name	**Karloff Negative**
Design	Peter Biľak, Pieter van Rosmalen, Nikola Djurek
Foundry	Typotheque
Year	2012
Category	(Static) Slab Serif

Karloff Negative was designed in 2012 by Peter Biľak, Pieter van Rosmalen, and Nikola Djurek. It was published by Typotheque, a type foundry based in the Netherlands.

It is part of the Karloff superfamily, which is based on an attempt to combine opposites into a coherent whole. Influenced by historical typefaces that were considered 'beautiful' (Bodoni, Didot) as well as 'degenerate' (Italienne-style typefaces), the designers first created two versions with the same skeleton. Each had the opposite contrast axis of the other. Interpolating between those two versions lead to a third family member, a neutral version whose design lay in the middle of the design space's extreme poles.

Karloff Negative is based on 'Italienne'-style Slab Serif typefaces that came about in the early 19th century. These stand out because of their unusual contrast-distribution model. Following their example, Karloff Negative's contrast is reversed. Its letters have thin vertical strokes while their horizontal strokes and serifs are designed to look extremely strong.

In addition to Karloff Negative (with a reversed, horizontal contrast axis), the Karloff superfamily includes Karloff Neutral (no contrast) and Karloff Positive (with a vertical contrast axis).

K

Whenever the black fox jumped the squirrel gazed suspiciously.

Name	**Karloff Neutral**
Design	Peter Biľak, Pieter van Rosmalen, Nikola Djurek
Foundry	Typotheque
Year	2012
Category	(Static) Slab Serif

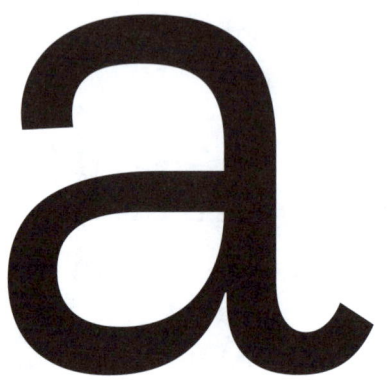

Karloff Neutral was designed in 2012 by Peter Biľak, Pieter van Rosmalen, and Nikola Djurek. It was published by Typotheque, a type foundry based in the Netherlands.

It is part of the Karloff superfamily, which is based on an attempt to combine opposites into a coherent whole. Influenced by historical typefaces that were considered 'beautiful' (Bodoni, Didot) as well as 'degenerate' (Italienne-style typefaces), the designers first created two versions with the same skeleton. Each had the opposite contrast axis of the other. Interpolating between those two versions lead to a third family member, a neutral version whose design lay in the middle of the design space's extreme poles.

Karloff Neutral is completely monolinear, so it has no stroke contrast – apart from a few optical adjustments. Its serifs are as thick as its stems and very much seem to be in the foreground, giving Karloff Neutral a robust character.

In addition to Karloff Neutral (no contrast), the Karloff superfamily includes Karloff Positive (with a vertical contrast axis) and Karloff Negative (with a reversed, horizontal contrast axis).

Whenever the black fox jumped the squirrel gazed suspiciously.

Name	**Karloff Positive**
Design	Peter Biľak, Pieter van Rosmalen, Nikola Djurek
Foundry	Typotheque
Year	2012
Category	(Static) Serif

Karloff Positive was designed in 2012 by Peter Bil'ak, Pieter van Rosmalen, and Nikola Djurek. It was published by Typotheque, a type foundry based in the Netherlands.

It is part of the Karloff superfamily, which is based on an attempt to combine opposites into a coherent whole. Influenced by historical typefaces that were considered 'beautiful' (Bodoni, Didot) as well as 'degenerate' (Italienne-style typefaces), the designers first created two versions with the same skeleton. Each had the opposite contrast axis of the other. Interpolating between those two versions lead to a third family member, a neutral version whose design lay in the middle of the design space's extreme poles.

Karloff Positive is based on Static Serif typefaces like Bodoni and Didot, which are considered expressions of beauty and elegance. Karloff Positive's stems are very strong and stand in contrast to the design's hairline strokes and fine, unbracketed serifs.

In addition to Karloff Positive (with a vertical contrast axis), the Karloff superfamily includes Karloff Neutral (no contrast) and Karloff Negative (with a reversed, horizontal contrast axis).

The quick brown
fox jumps over the
lazy dog.

Name	**Letter Gothic**
Design	Roger Roberson
Foundry	IBM	Monotype
Year	1962	1989
Category	(Dynamic) Sans Serif

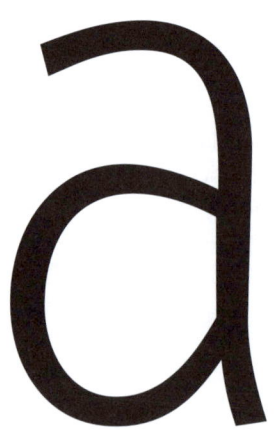

Letter Gothic was developed between 1956 and 1962 by Roger Roberson for IBM's 'Selectric' electric typewriter, whose changeable typing element – which was called a 'typeball' but looked a lot like a golf ball – allowed for the font installed in the machine to be switched. In 1989, a digital version of the typeface was published by Monotype.

Like other typewriter fonts, the letters in Letter Gothic all had the same width for mechanical reasons. However, unlike many other non-proportional typefaces, Letter Gothic has no serifs. The typeface is characterised by its condensed proportions and a tall x-height. The letterforms and counters open wide.

Despite the technical limitations that determined its appearance, Letter Gothic is a fairly uniform typeface. Like other monospace typefaces, using it creates a typical typewriter-looking effect. Nevertheless, this does not offer ideal reading conditions for longer texts.

Kris

The quick brown fox jumps over the lazy dog.

Name	Lo-Res
Design	Zuzana Licko
Foundry	Emigre
Year	1985	2001
Category	Display

Lo-Res was designed in 2001 by the American type designer Zuzana Licko and published by her digital type foundry Emigre.

The typeface is based on several Bitmap fonts that Licko originally drew in 1985 for use on computer screens, which at that time were very low-resolution, and dot-matrix printers. In 2001, Licko revised these and published them in a large type family under a new name. Her goal was to be able to display various type sizes at the same resolution that are all based on the same grid and which are all related to each other.

The Lo-Res 9 Narrow font shown here is based on a grid of 9 × 7 pixels. It is part of a series of pixel fonts with various weights (regular, bold), sizes (9, 12, 15, 21, 22, 28), widths (narrow, wide), and forms (with serifs, without serifs).

The explorative experimentation with technical restrictions and the resulting pixel aesthetic gives Lo-Res the distinctive character of early computer aesthetics.

Whenever the black fox jumped the squirrel gazed suspiciously.

Name	**Lucida Blackletter**
Design	Charles Bigelow, Kris Holmes
Foundry	Monotype
Year	1991
Category	Blackletter (Bastarda)

The Lucida superfamily was designed between 1984 and 1993 by the American type designers Charles Bigelow and Kris Holmes, then it was published by Monotype.

With Lucida, Bigelow and Holmes created a consistent superfamily with typefaces covering various categories: Sans Serif, Serif, Script, and Blackletter. Their goal was good on-screen legibility, even in small type sizes. The superfamily found widespread use through its implementation in Microsoft Office.

Lucida Blackletter is a Blackletter typeface that draws on the Schwabacher-style Bastarda in particular. Characteristic for that is the typeface's relatively broad width, forms that are strongly influenced by handwriting and a prominent horizontal stroke at the top of the lower-case 'g'. Also striking are the decorative strokes and dots in the capital letters, as well as the curved tapered ascenders in the lower-case.

With its old-fashioned, rustic and handwritten character, Lucida Blackletter is suitable for setting expressive-looking titles and other kinds of display typography. The typeface is complimented by the other members of the Lucida superfamily: Lucida Bright, Lucida Calligraphy, Lucida Console, Lucida Fax, Lucida Grande, Lucida Handwriting, Lucida Sans, Lucida Sans Typewriter, and Lucida Serif.

THE QUICK BROWN FOX JUMPS OVER THE LAZY DOG.

Name	Lÿno Jean
Design	Karl Nawrot, Radim Peško
Foundry	RP Digital Type Foundry
Year	2010
Category	Display

Lÿno was designed by Karl Nawrot and Radim Peško between 2009 and 2012 for Peško's RP Digital Type Foundry.

The typeface first appeared in 2010 inside a brochure entitled *Newer Alphabets* – a reference to Wim Crouwel's New Alphabet. Its goal was to break norms with the unusual letter shapes in the typeface's four versions.

Those four styles are each based on specific sources of inspiration, from which the fonts' names are also drawn: Ulys (inspired by Ulysses 31) is constructed solely out of straight lines, making it look very edgy and aggressive. Stan (inspired by Stanley Kubrick) combines features from Ulys with round letterforms, leading to unusual shapes and proportions. In Jean (inspired by Jean Arp) the letters have running and dripping forms that have been combined with geometric aspects. Walt (inspired by Walt Disney) is based on the Disney logo, which is abstracted in this font's design.

With its exceptional letterforms and very unusual character, Lÿno is particularly suitable for use in large type sizes and poster design. Lÿno only has capital letters; instead of lower-case letters, typing those keys gives users alternate versions of the upper-case letters.

Whenever the black fox jumped the squirrel gazed suspiciously.

Name	Meta
Design	Erik Spiekermann
Foundry	FontFont (Monotype)
Year	1991
Category	(Dynamic) Sans Serif

FF Meta was designed by the German designer and typographer Erik Spiekermann. He published it through his then newly established FontFont foundry in 1991.

The typeface originated in 1985 when Spiekermann proposed a new corporate typeface for the West German postal service. In the end, they did not use it, so he developed it into a commercial product. During the typeface's development, a great deal of emphasis was put on its having good legibility, economy of space, and an independent character.

Formally, Meta is distinguished by its Humanistic character. It has mild stroke contrast, its letter-forms and their counters are wide open. The pro-portions of its capitals and lower-case letters are narrow. All in all, its letters are quite differentiated from one another, making text set in the typeface pleasantly readable.

In addition to its friendly and clear character, Meta stands out because of how extensive it is as a family. It has a variety of styles and the type system was even extended in 2007 to include FF Meta Serif. In 2018 FF Meta Variable was published, too. Since it first appeared on the market, Meta has been popular, especially in the realm of corporate design.

Whenever the black fox jumped the squirrel gazed suspiciously.

Name	**Minérale**
Design	Thomas Huot-Marchand
Foundry	205TF
Year	2018
Category	Display

Minérale was designed by the French type designer Thomas Huot-Marchand and published by 205TF in 2018.

The contrast distribution of Minérale's letters is extraordinary. Their basic construction is based on stems whose sides cross in the middle. The principle of having tapered stems dates back to typefaces like Optima – at least – but in Minérale, the feature is driven to extremes. In Minérale's heavier weights, this results in geometric, almost abstract-looking letterforms. In the lighter weights, the effect is less prominent.

Since Minérale is a variable font, it is possible to seamlessly vary the stroke thickness (and with it, the letterforms' contrast). Minérale's unusual structure makes it a pioneering contribution to the new variable font format.

Whenever the black fox jumped the squirrel gazed suspiciously.

Name	Minion
Design	Robert Slimbach
Foundry	Adobe
Year	1989
Category	(Dynamic) Serif

Minion was designed by the American type designer Robert Slimbach and published by Adobe in 1989.

Influenced by various typeface models from the Renaissance, Minion was conceived as a space-saving design with optimal legibility.

Openness, bright colour, and Minion's even pattern in text characterise the typeface. Its open letterforms make Minion easier to read, too, and give the design a pleasant, reserved personality. The typeface's name can be traced back to the historical term of a specific size of type in letter-press printing. At that time, 'Minion' referred to fonts that were about 7pt in size.

Due to the properties described, Minion is ideal for use in body text. Its large number of extensions – including with a variety of weights and styles – allow for a range of options. For instance, Minion's fonts include small caps and ornaments, and the family includes styles for different optical sizes.

Carol

The quick br■wn f■x jumps ■ver the lazy d■g.

Name	Minuscule
Design	Thomas Huot-Marchand
Foundry	205TF
Year	2005
Category	Display

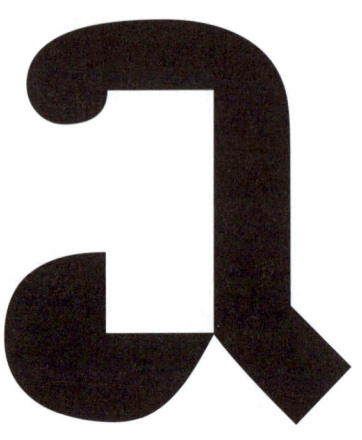

Minuscule was designed in 2005 by the French type designer Thomas Huot-Marchand and published by the foundry 256TM.

With Minuscule, Huot-Marchand pursued the goal of developing a scientifically-sound typeface for small sizes, inspired by the work of the ophthalmologist Émile Javal from 1905. Minuscule's various styles are optimised for – and named after – specific point sizes (e.g., 6, 5, 4, 3, and 2 pt).

As the size becomes smaller, optical adjustments become more extreme. The letterforms' contours become more simplified, the x-height gets taller, and ascenders and descenders get shorter. Strongly-emphasised ink-traps optical prevent strokes from tapering. In Minuscule's smallest style, for 2 pt type, the letterforms have been very simplified. For instance, the 'o' is just a single black square. Thanks to its design concept, Minuscule is ideal for use in very small sizes. Due to its striking form, it has been classified here among the Display fonts, although it is based on a Dynamic Serif.

Whenever the black fox jumped the squirrel gazed suspiciously.

Name	**Mistral**
Design	Roger Excoffon
Foundry	Fonderie Olive
Year	1953
Category	Handwritten (Script)

Mistral was designed by the French graphic designer and typographer Roger Excoffon in 1953. The typeface was distributed by the Fonderie Olive.

With Mistral, Excoffon was looking for a solution to the problem of how to design a connected Script-style typeface that would be convincing. Due to the technical restrictions that the rectilinearity of metal type brought, and the accompanying difficulty of having part of a letter protrude into the 'space' of another, this had not yet been solved. After trying out different attempts, Excoffon found a way to base Mistral on his handwriting.

The structure of the typeface is reminiscent of writing with a felt-tip or ballpoint pen. Due to the

challenge of connecting letters to one another,
there is no fixed placement of the letters' baseline
and x-height – making it even more like handwriting.
However, there is a fixed vertical position of the
places where the lower-case letters join up.
This ensures that each letter can be combined with
every other. Excoffon also developed a range
of ligatures, as well as alternate letters, to make the
typeface seem more random and similar to how
handwriting looks.

Even though the problems from that time can be
solved today with OpenType features, Mistral
was a masterpiece when it was published, and it is
still one of the most-used script typefaces.

Whenever the black fox jumped the squirrel gazed suspiciously.

Name	Mrs Eaves
Design	Zuzana Licko
Foundry	Emigre
Year	1996
Category	(Dynamic) Serif

Mrs Eaves was designed by the American type designer Zuzana Licko and published by Emigre in 1996.

Inspired by the typefaces from John Baskerville, Mrs Eaves is more than just a typeface revival. Emigre was very early on the scene when it came to developing and distributing digital fonts. However, Licko found that many typeface revivals looked too smooth when compared to prints made with the metal types that had inspired them. They conveyed little of the original character those typefaces had.

With Mrs Eaves, Licko picked up on the impression of the printed image and referenced how ink was originally distributed, both when it came to stroke contrast, as well as in the contours. Mrs Eaves features emphasised strokes, an almost upright contrast axis, and a low x-height. The typeface is named after Sarah Eaves, Baskerville's wife and business partner, who continued Baskerville's work after his death.

With its dynamic character, Mrs Eaves is particularly suitable for long passages of texts intended for immersive reading.

Whenever the black fox jumped the squirrel gazed suspiciously.

Name	National
Design	Kris Sowersby
Foundry	Klim Type Foundry
Year	2007
Category	(Dynamic) Sans Serif

National was developed by the New Zealand type designer Kris Sowersby for the Klim Type Foundry in 2007.

Formally, National is based on the early Sans Serif typefaces that appeared at the end of the 19th and the beginning of the 20th century, like Akzidenz Grotesk. Those influences are combined with Humanistic traits. Features of National's design include its relatively open forms, its gradual curves and stroke terminals, moderate ascenders and descenders, and the low height of its capitals.

These attributes give National a warm character. The typeface is suitable for body text as well as for use in large sizes.

Uli

Fhe quict broun foi junpb ouer the Lupy dod..

N

Fonts A → Z

Name	New Alphabet
Design	Wim Crouwel
Foundry	The Foundry (Monotype)
Year	1967	1997
Category	Display

The New Alphabet was created by the Dutch graphic designer Wim Crouwel in 1967. He published it as a type specimen. In 1997, The Foundry produced a digital revival as a typeface.

Crouwel's observations on technical restrictions present at the beginning of digital typesetting formed the conceptual basis of the New Alphabet. The machines at that time could only store representations of horizontal and vertical elements on a dot matrix.

His experimental approach led Crouwel to new forms for the new technology. The result was a modular lower-case alphabet based on a 5 × 9 grid. Letters only consisted of horizontal and vertical lines, and their outer corners were cut off at 45-degree angles. That formal limitation created reduced letterforms that went to the limits of recognizability.

In Crouwel's own words, the New Alphabet was 'not meant to be used', but was rather a contribution to the impact of contemporary technology on typographic tradition.

Whenever the black fox jumped the squirrel gazed suspiciously.

Name	News Gothic
Design	Morris Fuller Benton
Foundry	American Type Founders
Year	1908
Category	(Transitional) Sans Serif

News Gothic was designed by the American type designer Morris Fuller Benton and published by the American Type Founders Company in 1908.

Against the background of a rapid increase in newspaper and magazine circulation at the beginning of the 20th century, News Gothic was designed with the particular aim of saving space and being very legible. This allowed it to be used in those media as widely as possible.

Like other American Sans Serifs, including Franklin Gothic, one of the hallmarks of the News Gothic typeface is that it has characteristic letterforms inspired by Serif typefaces. For instance, it has double-storey forms for the lower-case 'a' and 'g'.

Its letters are slightly open and their x-height is quite tall. Both of those features contribute to the typeface having a good degree of legibility. News Gothic's letters have hardly any stroke contrast. Together with their relatively short ascenders and descenders, this helps create a uniform pattern in texts.

Thanks to its good legibility and narrow running width, News Gothic is still suitable for use in applications where space is tight, including in newspaper and magazine design.

The quick brown fox jumps over the lazy dog.

Name	Nitti
Design	Pieter van Rosmalen
Foundry	Bold Monday
Year	2008
Category	(Static) Sans Serif

Nitti was designed in 2008 by the Dutch type designer Pieter van Rosmalen and published by Bold Monday.

Formally, it is inspired by typewriter typefaces. Like so many of those, Nitti is a non-proportional typeface (also called a 'fixed-width' or 'mono-space' typeface). The letterforms are also inspired by the designs of early Sans Serif typefaces from the 19th century. Nitti is characterised by low stroke-contrast and a tall x-height. The balanced proportions of its capitals and lower-case contribute to the typeface's uniformity and help it ensure good legibility.

The typeface is complemented by the proportionally-spaced Nitti Grotesk. The superfamily also has a display variant named Nitti Mostro. Nitti supports the Latin, Greek, Cyrillic, and Hebrew scripts. Its extensive character set covers a large repertoire of languages, too.

Eric

Whenever the black fox jumped the squirrel gazed suspiciously.

Name	Noe Display
Design	Lauri Toikka, Florian Schick
Foundry	Schick Toikka
Year	2013
Category	(Static) Serif

Noe Display was designed by the type designers Lauri Toikka and Florian Schick in 2013. They published it through their type foundry Schick Toikka. It is part of the Noe superfamily.

The typeface began as part of Lauri Toikka's graduation project while he studied on the Type and Media course at the Royal Academy of Art (KABK) in The Hague. Conceptually and formally, Noe Display is based on historical Static Serif typefaces.

This design lineage is particularly visible in Noe Display's vertical contrast axis and the high degree of contrast between its letters' strong stems and fine hairline strokes. In particular, the treatment of the typeface's out-strokes is important: the strokes taper to a point or end in triangular terminals. These terminals can also be found in the letters' wedge-shaped, unbracketed serifs. These properties are particularly noticeable in the lower-case 'a', 'c', 'f', 'g', 'r', and 's'.

Due to its pointed, wedge-shaped serifs and their strong stroke contrast, Noe Display attracts attention and is particularly suited for expressive display applications and other large-sized uses. The Noe superfamily also includes a variant optimised for body text: Noe Text.

Whenever the black fox jumped the squirrel gazed suspiciously.

Name	Noe Text
Design	Lauri Toikka, Florian Schick
Foundry	Schick Toikka
Year	2015
Category	(Dynamic) Serif

Noe Text comes from the type designers Lauri Toikka and Florian Schick. In 2015, they published it through their type foundry Schick Toikka as part of the Noe superfamily.

Usually, typefaces for reading sizes are designed first, before suitable display variations are available to join them. When it came to Noe, however, the opposite is true. Schick Toikka developed Noe Display first. Two years later, they brought out a matching text version that ensures good readability thanks to its low stroke contrast, slightly inclined contrast axis, and wedge-shaped serifs. Nevertheless, Noe Text remains true to the strong character of the original display design.

In particular, the treatment of the typeface's outstrokes is important for Noe's design: the strokes taper to a point or end in triangular terminals. Those terminals can also be found in the letters' wedge-shaped, unbracketed serifs. These properties are particularly noticeable in the lower-case 'a', 'c', 'f', 'g', 'r', and 's'.

Per its conception, Noe Text is particularly suitable for body text and for setting other long passages of text. If you are looking for an expressive headline-typeface to match, combine Noe Text with Noe Display.

Whenever the black fox jumped the squirrel gazed suspiciously.

Name	Nordvest
Design	Nina Stössinger
Foundry	Monokrom
Year	2016
Category	(Static) Slab Serif

Nordvest comes from the Swiss type designer Nina Stössinger. It was published by the Norwegian foundry Monokrom in 2016.

Stössinger developed Nordvest based on her studies of typefaces with reverse contrast, a genre that includes both display typefaces with a 'Western look' and more subtle examples like Antique Olive. Nevertheless, she positioned Nordvest to work much more as a text typeface than as a display typeface.

Nordvest features all the characteristics of a reversed-contrast typeface: the emphasis is on the horizontals, horizontal strokes, and curves that are thicker than the vertical stems, etc. Nordvest's triangular slab serifs reinforce this. Despite its unusual contrast-distribution model, Nordvest creates a calm pattern in texts and remains easy and pleasant to read.

Due to its unusual constriction, Nordvest has a high recognition value and a distinctive character.

Simon

Whenever the black fox jumped the squirrel gazed suspiciously.

Name	Noto Sans
Design	Google
Foundry	Google Fonts
Year	2013
Category	(Dynamic) Sans Serif

Noto Sans is part of an extensive superfamily commissioned by Google and published in 2013.

Google's goal with Noto Sans was to cover all writing systems contained in Unicode. The typeface is constantly being expanded and already supports more than 500 languages, including languages written with European as well as Asian and African scripts, plus scripts used in the Middle East and India. Minority languages and historical writing systems are also supported to a certain degree.

To keep its high degree of compatibility with as many scripts as possible, Noto Sans is characterised by a relatively neutral design language. Its letterforms are open, its x-height is quite tall, and its ascenders

reach up above the height of the capital letters, while its descenders are shorter. Most stroke terminals end in either a vertical or horizontal. Noto Sans has hardly any visible stroke contrast. All of these features give it a high degree of legibility in body text.

The Noto Sans fonts are available free of charge under the Open Font License. Due to its immense character set and its having been optimised for on-screen reading, the fonts are particularly suited for multilingual applications and web design. A companion with serifs – called Noto Serif – is also in development and was first published in 2017.

Whenever the black fox jumped the squirrel gazed suspiciously.

Name	Engravers Old English
Design	Morris Fuller Benton (1901), Monotype (2001)
Foundry	ATF	Monotype
Year	1901	2001
Category	Blackletter (Textura)

Old English is based on a typeface of William Caslon's from 1734. The typeface shown here, Engravers Old English, was designed by Morris Fuller Benton and published by ATF in 1901. A digital adaption of the typeface was published by Monotype in 2001.

From a classification angle, Old English is a Blackletter typeface belonging to the Textura subcategory. Its design origins are in Gothic-era handwriting styles. In the days when printing was still new in Western and Central Europe, this was a very common style.

As is typical of Textura-style typefaces, Old English is characterised by a strong geometrical fracturing of the letterforms' strokes. Old English's lower-case letters are quite narrow, leading to a dense, black pattern in texts. Its strong handwritten character is also striking; in particular, you notice it in the doubled strokes and ornamented counters inside the typeface's swashed capitals. Both the lower-case 'a' and the capital 'A' are particularly recognis-able.

With its historical appearance and its decorative capitals, Old English is suitable for setting expres-sive headlines and other display applications.

Whenever the black fox jumped the squirrel gazed suspiciously.

Name	Optima
Design	Hermann Zapf
Foundry	Stempel (Monotype)
Year	1958
Category	(Dynamic) Sans Serif

Optima was designed by Hermann Zapf between about 1952 and 1955. D. Stempel AG published it as foundry type and machine-setting matrices in 1958. In 2003, Akira Kobayashi revised the typeface together with Zapf; they published it as Optima Nova.

For Optima's design, Zapf was inspired by Renaissance inscriptions in Florence. While its letters followed the structure of Ancient Roman lettering, they did not have serifs. Impressed by this, Zapf decided to develop an easy-to-read Sans Serif typeface that would stand out from the Grotesk offerings that were popular at the time. Optima is characterised by high stroke contrast (an innovation in Sans Serif type back then).

Also striking are the letterforms' stems, which
taper in the middle. This is reminiscent of
inscriptional lettering styles from antiquity, too.
The proportions of Optima's capital letters
are borrowed from Ancient Roman models. On the
other hand, the elegant stroke pattern in the
lower-case letters' design comes from Renaissance
models. Wide apertures help make Optima's
letterforms very legible.

Thanks to its commonality with design elements
otherwise found in Dynamic Serif typefaces,
Optima is particularly suitable for use in body text.
It can also be used to set expressive titles and
other display applications.

The quick brown fox jumps over the lazy dog.

Name	Orientation
Design	Sandrine Nugue
Foundry	Commercial Type
Year	2018
Category	Display

Orientation comes from the French type designer Sandrine Nugue. It was published by the Commercial Type foundry in 2018.

The typeface was originally commissioned as a stencil design for the signage system in a student dormitory. Afterwards, Nugue expanded the typeface and made it commercially available. Among other things, Orientation's strong geometrically-reduced character is due to its being able to be applied directly onto buildings by using stencils. Indeed, the typeface's functionality in stencils explains the characteristic cuts in its letters, which you can find on the 'a' or the 'e'.

With strong geometric, almost abstract letterforms and an expressive character, Orientation is particularly suitable for use in headlines, for large single words, or display applications.

The quick brown fox jumps over the lazy dog.

Name	Pareto
Design	Johannes Breyer, Fabian Harb, Erkin Karamemet
Foundry	Dinamo
Year	2016
Category	Display

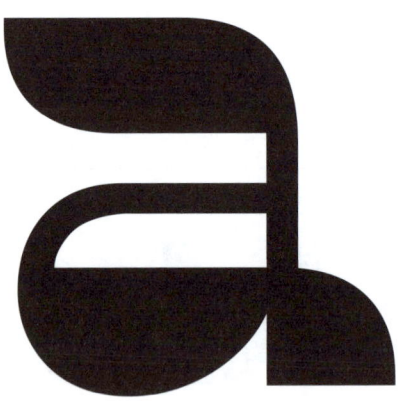

Pareto was designed by Johannes Breyer, Fabian Harb, and Erkin Karamemet for the Swiss foundry Dinamo in 2016.

With its reverse contrast and strongly Geometric Slab Serifs, this design looks like a contemporary version of so-called 'Italienne' or Western typefaces. Pareto has three variants, which differ from one another in the shapes of their serifs. These are triangular, rectangular, and semicircular, respectively. Their letterforms have strong geometric constructions. Together with their high degree of reversed contrast and striking serif forms, that geometry gives the typeface its particularly unique character.

Thanks to the above-mentioned properties, Pareto is particularly suitable for use in poster-sized headlines and other display applications.

Whenever the black fox jumped the squirrel gazed suspiciously.

Name	Pensum
Design	Nils Thomsen
Foundry	TypeMates
Year	2016
Category	(Dynamic) Serif

Pensum Pro was developed by the German type designer Nils Thomsen for the TypeMates foundry in 2016.

Inspired by exercises with broad pens and brushes he undertook while studying on the Type and Media master's degree course at the Royal Academy of Art (KABK) in The Hague, Thomsen created Pensum as a text typeface influenced by traditional writing instruments.

The letters in Pensum are wide open. Plus, they have a tall x-height and low contrast. These properties ensure good legibility, especially in small text sizes. Strokes tapering towards the stems contribute to the typeface's pattern in text at small sizes, too; in large sizes, these emphasise the typeface's character. In particular, Pensum's lower-case 'e' is a highly recognisable letter.

Due to the properties mentioned above, Pensum is an excellent choice for use in body text. Its large character sets also allow it to be used for setting many other languages.

Lara

Whenever the black fox jumped the squirrel gazed suspiciously.

Name	Ping
Design	Peter Bil'ak, Nikola Djurek et al.
Foundry	Typotheque
Year	2019
Category	(Geometric) Sans Serif

Ping was created by a team of designers including Peter Bil'ak and Nikola Djurek. The typeface was published by the Typotheque foundry in the Netherlands in 2019.

By combining influence from Geometric Sans Serifs like Futura and Erbar with the approach of building letters with as few strokes as possible, Ping is similar to a handwriting system. This concept is particularly notable in lower-case letters like the 'a', 'b', 'd', 'g', and 'p'. The influence of Humanistic handwriting styles can also be recognised in the lower-case letters' wide-open counters. Together with a tall x-height and short ascenders and descenders, these features contribute to Ping's being quite legible.

Aside from OpenType features like small caps and a novel unicase functionality, Ping's extensive character set supports a lot of different writing systems. These were included in the design from the start so that Ping could be a cross-border, internationally-usable typeface.

With a geometric character combined with Humanistic features, Ping is suitable for use in both body text as well as for headlines and other display applications.

Whenever the black fox jumped the squirrel gazed suspiciously.

Name	**Replica**
Design	Dimitri Bruni, Manuel Krebs
Foundry	Lineto
Year	2008
Category	(Static) Sans Serif

Coming from Dimitri Bruni and Manuel Krebs
of the Swiss design studio Norm, LL Replica was
published by the foundry Lineto in 2008.

Replica is a reinterpretation of modernist Sans
Serif typefaces like Helvetica. The letterforms are
constructed on a deliberately-reduced grid.
All stroke endings and transitions are chamfered.
This gives the typeface an optical softness, despite its geometric construction. It is also Replica's
most-striking characteristic, especially in larger
type sizes.

Due to their shortened diagonals, Replica's letters
fit together well, forming a uniform pattern in
text. This is abetted by the typeface's homogenous
stroke thickness. Its letterforms are closed
and strokes end either in verticals or horizontals.

Since its publication, Replica has been very popular.

Herb

Whenever the black fox jumped the squirrel gazed suspiciously.

Name	Rockwell
Design	Frank Hinman Pierpont
Foundry	Monotype
Year	1934
Category	(Geometric) Slab Serif

Rockwell was developed by the American typographer and engineer Frank Hinman Pierpont for the Monotype typesetting-machine manufacturing company in 1934.

19th-century wood types served as the inspiration for Rockwell's design. Rockwell is also a rationalisation and reduction of an older type design Monotype published under the name Series 173 in 1913.

The Rockwell typeface's construction is mainly geometric, but features can be found that reference its historical models, such as the double-storey form of the lower-case 'a'. Also characteristic are the upper serifs on Rockwell's capital 'A' and several round letters like 'c', 'C', and 'G'.

Rockwell belongs to the cadre of Geometric Slab Serif typefaces that began appearing in the 1930s. These drew on the popularity of the Geometric Sans Serif typefaces from the 1920s, like Futura and Kabel. They supplemented those geometric designs with serifs. Together with Memphis, Rockwell is one of the most well-known representatives of its category.

Whenever the black fox jumped the squirrel gazed suspiciously.

Name	Rotis Sans Serif
Design	Otl Aicher
Foundry	Agfa, Linotype (Monotype)
Year	1988
Category	(Dynamic) Sans Serif

Rotis Sans Serif is part of the Rotis superfamily created by the German graphic designer Otl Aicher and published in 1988. It is one of the first typographic superfamilies to have been made.

Aicher's concept was to develop a series of typefaces that were consistent with each other, which could realise the same even grey colour in text, even though they differ enough through their various characteristics that they can each be used to transport different content.

The Rotis superfamily's typefaces have a mild degree of stroke contrast, their letters have very wide open apertures, and their x-heights are relatively tall. These features ensure good legibility. The letters run rather condensed, and their terminals are always either horizontal or vertical. A characteristic feature of the Rotis typefaces is the lower-case 'e', with its small, very highly-posited counter.

Rotis has enjoyed great popularity since its publication. The typeface is suitable for use both in body text as well as for headlines and brand communication. Rotis Sans Serif is supplemented by the other typefaces in the Rotis superfamily: Rotis Semi Sans, Rotis Semi Serif, and Rotis Serif.

Whenever the black fox jumped the squirrel gazed suspiciously.

Name	Rotis Serif
Design	Otl Aicher
Foundry	Agfa, Linotype (Monotype)
Year	1988
Category	(Dynamic) Serif

Rotis Serif is part of the Rotis superfamily created by the German graphic designer Otl Aicher and published in 1988. It is one of the first typographic superfamilies to have been made.

Aicher's concept was to develop a series of typefaces that were consistent with each other, which could realise the same even grey colour in text, even though they differ enough through their various characteristics that they can each be used to transport different content.

The Rotis superfamily's typefaces have a mild degree of stroke contrast, their letters have very wide open apertures, and their x-heights are relatively tall. These features ensure good legibility. The letters run rather condensed, and their terminals are always either horizontal or vertical. A characteristic feature of the Rotis typefaces is the lower-case 'e', with its small, very highly-posited counter.

Rotis has enjoyed great popularity since its publication. The typeface is suitable for use both in body text as well as for headlines and brand communication. Rotis Serif is supplemented by the other typefaces in the Rotis superfamily: Rotis Semi Serif, Rotis Semi Sans, and Rotis Sans Serif.

Whenever the black fox jumped the squirrel gazed suspiciously.

Name	**Sabon**
Design	Jan Tschichold
Foundry	Stempel, Linotype (Monotype)
Year	1964
Category	(Dynamic) Serif

Sabon is a Dynamic Serif typeface created in 1964 by the Swiss book designer and typographer Jan Tschichold. He carried out the work under commission from Linotype, Monotype, and the D. Stempel AG.

Against the background of the many technical changes that were underway in the printing process during in the 1960s, the type companies Linotype, Monotype and D. Stempel AG commissioned Tschichold to design a typeface that would function across all three of their different typesetting systems (e.g., the Linotype and Monotype hot-metal casting machines, as well as hand-setting fonts that Stempel cast). No matter which method would be used for composing type, the fonts should deliver the same text pattern in print. Tschichold developed Sabon based on a type specimen sheet from 1592 that showed a number of typefaces attributed to Claude Garamont and Robert Granjon. He also took the influence of the letter-press printing technique into account and designed a stroke-contrast system that would look balanced on the page. Sabon has asymmetrical serifs and a moderate degree of stroke contrast. Its ascenders reach up past the tops of the capital letters, and its descenders are short. Another characteristic feature of Sabon's letters is that they are soft and round. The apertures in letters like 'a' and 'e' are wide open, which contributes to good legibility.

Due to its humanistic qualities and its modern revisions, Sabon is one of the most relied upon typefaces to use for setting long passages of text intended for immersive reading.

Firmin

Whenever the black fox jumped the squirrel gazed suspiciously.

Name	San Marco
Design	Karlgeorg Hoefer
Foundry	Linotype (Monotype)
Year	1991
Category	Blackletter (Rotunda)

San Marco comes from the German calligrapher and type designer Karlgeorg Hoefer. It was published by the Linotype company in 1991.

The typeface was created as part of the 'Type before Gutenberg' programme that Linotype had initiated, in which well-known calligraphers were invited to reinterpret historical handwriting styles practised before printing had been invented.

San Marco was modelled on Rotunda types cut by Nicolas Jenson in Venice around 1470. Above all, Hoefer's design is characterised by its strong handwritten character, which is based on forms written with a broad pen. Like other Rotunda typefaces, the broken elements in the letterforms' strokes are not as prominent as in other categories of Blackletter. The lower-case letters are rounder, have simpler designs, and strokes end without elaborate terminal forms. Also noteworthy are the very swashy capitals, decorated with double strokes.

Thanks to San Marco's curved, calligraphic forms, the typeface attracts a lot of attention. Because of its clear and direct strokes, Sans Marco is very legible. It is ideal for use in expressive headlines and other display applications.

Whenever the black fox jumped the squirrel gazed suspiciously.

Name	**SangBleu Empire**
Design	Swiss Typefaces
Foundry	Swiss Typefaces
Year	2017
Category	(Static) Serif

SangBleu Empire was made and published by the type design studio Swiss Typefaces (from Switzerland) in 2017. It is part of the SangBleu superfamily.

The SangBleu superfamily comprises four Serif typefaces plus a Sans Serif, which are each based on a similar skeleton. Nevertheless, they differ from one another in the exact historical and stylistic elements they use. Most of the typefaces can be classified following the Static Principle of Form but each of them handles stroke contrast, serif shapes and letterform details differently.

From a historical perspective, SangBleu Empire is partially inspired by transitional typefaces such as the Romain du Roi, but, as opposed to other members of the SangBleu superfamily, its design has also been influenced by the Didot typefaces. That late-18th/early-19th century model is characterised above all by the strong contrast between thick stems and hairline strokes. Their in-strokes have sharp edges; their out-strokes do, too. Stems end in hairline serifs placed at right angles to the main strokes. The contrast between thick and thin elements is particularly striking, as is the contrast between the typeface's rounded and angular forms.

With its elegant shapes and strong contrast – both in terms of stroke thickness and in between rounds and straight lines – SangBleu Empire is well suited for use in expressive headlines and other large-sized display applications. SangBleu Empire may be combined with other typefaces from its superfamily: SangBleu Kingdom, Republic, Versailles, and Sunrise.

Whenever the black fox jumped the squirrel gazed suspiciously.

Name	**SangBleu Sunrise**
Design	Swiss Typefaces
Foundry	Swiss Typefaces
Year	2017
Category	(Static) Sans Serif

SangBleu Sunrise was made and published by the type design studio Swiss Typefaces (from Switzerland) in 2017. It is part of the SangBleu superfamily.

SangBleu Sunrise is the only typeface in the SangBleu superfamily without serifs. While SangBleu Sunrise shares the strong contrast and other prominent features making up the superfamily's other styles, it is more reduced formally. In that sense, it can be described as having the whole superfamily's essence, reduced down into Sans Serif form.

By being a Sans Serif with unusually-high contrast, SangBleu Sunrise definitely attracts attention. It is therefore particularly suitable for use in expressive headlines and other display applications, but it can also be used for setting a moderate amount of body text. SangBleu Sunrise may be combined with other typefaces from its superfamily: SangBleu Empire, Kingdom, Republic, and Versailles.

Whenever the black fox jumped the squirrel gazed suspiciously.

Name	Scala
Design	Martin Majoor
Foundry	FontFont (Monotype)
Year	1991
Category	(Dynamic) Serif

Scala comes from the Dutch graphic designer and type designer Martin Majoor, who published the typeface with the FontFont foundry in 1991.

The Scala superfamily – including Scala and the later-designed Scala Sans – primarily arose from Majoor's view that the fonts then available for the Apple Macintosh did not have the necessary typographic options. The available options were just not fully-developed enough. As part of a design he developed for the 'Muziekcentrum Vredenburg', he implemented Scala as a solution to that problem.

Scala follows the Dynamic Principle of Form. Its contrast axis is therefore inclined and its letterforms are wide open. The bottom serifs are rectangular and strongly emphasised, while the top serifs are set onto the stems at an angle. The strong serifs give the capital letters an almost Slab Serif character, and the contrast between soft, round, and angular forms is particularly noticeable in the lower-case. The open counters of the 'b', 'q', and 'p' are striking as well.

For Majoor to meet his original need for typographic enhancements, Scala received small caps and several numeral variants. In 1994, Majoor's Sans Serif companion to Scala was also published: Scala Sans.

Whenever the black fox jumped the squirrel gazed suspiciously.

Name	Scala Sans
Design	Martin Majoor
Foundry	FontFont (Monotype)
Year	1994
Category	(Dynamic) Sans Serif

Scala Sans comes from the Dutch graphic designer and type designer Martin Majoor. He published the typeface with the FontFont foundry in 1994. It is the Sans Serif companion to his Scala typeface, published in 1991.

The Scala superfamily primarily arose from Majoor's view that the fonts then available for the Apple Macintosh did not have the necessary typographic options. The available options were just not fully-developed enough. As part of a design he developed for the 'Muziekcentrum Vredenburg', he implemented Scala as a solution to that problem.

Like Scala, Scala Sans follows the Dynamic Principle of Form, and its letters are wide open. In contrast to Scala, Scala Sans has hardly any stroke contrast. Its letterforms' contours are simplified and reduced when compared with Scala's.

With its dynamic properties, Scala Sans is ideally suited as a typeface for setting body text. It also works well in combination with Scala.

Indra

Whenever the black fox jumped the squirrel gazed suspiciously.

Name	Sectra
Design	Dominik Huber, Marc Kappeler, Noël Leu
Foundry	Grilli Type
Year	2013
Category	(Dynamic) Serif

GT Sectra was designed by Dominik Huber, Marc Kappeler, and Noël Leu for the *Reportagen* magazine and published by Grilli Type in 2013.

The design of the Sectra typeface arose out of an attempt to combine contemporary, constructed elements with a calligraphic character. The letters are based on a handwritten framework, which is changed by the cutting off of (and the abstraction of) individual details. This creates unusual forms – like terminals that are angular in shape, instead of drawn to look like teardrops. Other examples include the arches, whose shapes feature additional angles, giving them the appearance of having been cut or broken.

The rather tall x-height, moderate ascenders and descenders, and relatively narrow capital letters all contribute to Sectra having a good flow in text. Ink-traps have also been built into the letterforms, which emphasise the typeface's character in larger type sizes.

Despite its calligraphic properties, Sectra manages to retain a contemporary and distinctive character and is suitable both for use in setting body text as well as headlines and other display applications. The text version is complemented by a fine version and a display style, which has increased contrast and exaggerated characteristic features.

The quick brown
fox jumps over the
lazy dog.

Name	Simple
Design	Manuel Krebs, Dimitri Bruni
Foundry	Lineto
Year	2002
Category	(Geometric) Sans Serif

LL Simple was developed in 2002 by Manuel Krebs and Dimitri Bruni of the Swiss design studio Norm for their book *The Things*. The typeface was then published by Lineto.

The basis of Simple was the Normetica typeface, which the design studio had developed a year earlier. Like Normetica, Simple is monospaced and its letters are geometrically constructed. In those kinds of typefaces, individual letters have to all be adjusted to share the same width, which for many narrow letters requires adding or extending existing horizontal strokes. This is particularly noticeable in the 'f', 'i', and 'r', as well as in wide letters like the 'm' and 'w'.

Despite its uniform character width, Simple retains good legibility in body text and is also very suitable for headlines.

Peter

S

Whenever the black fox jumped the squirrel gazed suspiciously.

Name	**Spectral**
Design	Jean-Baptiste Levée
Foundry	Production Type
Year	2017
Category	(Dynamic) Serif

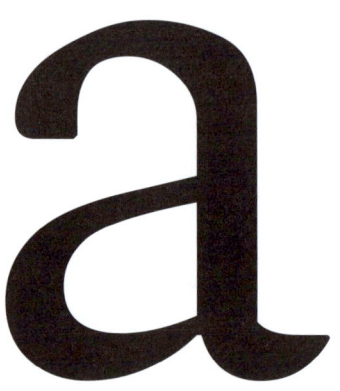

Google commissioned Spectral from the French type designer Jean-Baptiste Levée of Production Type in 2017.

Designed and optimised for use on screen and in texts intended for immersive reading, Spectral is included as one of the standard fonts installed in Google Docs, Sheets, and Slides. Spectral is also available free of charge under the Open Font License.

Spectral is characterised by its pointed, wedge-shaped serifs, which give the typeface a solid a filigree character at the same time. Its contrast axis is only slightly inclined and its letterforms are open, as can be seen in the 'e' and 'a'. Its ascenders reach up past the tops of the capital letters, and the lengths of its descenders are moderate. These attributes promote a high degree of legibility in body text.

Thanks to its being optimised for on-screen use, Spectral is particularly suitable for setting long amounts of text for reading online. It also has a Cyrillic character set and thus covers an exceptionally wide range of languages.

Whenever the black fox jumped the squirrel gazed suspiciously.

Name	Swift
Design	Gerard Unger
Foundry	Rudolf Hell	Linotype (Monotype)
Year	1987	2009
Category	(Dynamic) Serif

Swift was created by the Dutch graphic designer and type designer Gerard Unger for Rudolf Hell, who first published it in 1987. The typeface was revised and re-released in 1995 as Swift 2.0 and again as Neue Swift in 2009.

Unger originally designed Swift for use in printed newspapers. Due to their being printed rapidly on low-quality stock, text in newspapers often appears quite coarse.

Swift is characterised by very solid letter construction. Its characters feature tall x-heights and are wide open. These elements help make it very legible, even in small type sizes. Its serifs are strong and wedge-shaped, giving Swift a stable character. Nevertheless – due to its Humanistic influence – the typeface also conveys dynamism and a certain easiness.

Thanks to its stable construction and optimisation for newspaper printing, Swift is excellently suitable for use in long passages of body text.

Mike

Whenever the black fox jumped the squirrel gazed suspiciously.

Name	Syntax
Design	Hans Eduard Meier
Foundry	Stempel	Linotype (Monotype)
Year	1969	2000
Category	(Dynamic) Sans Serif

Syntax was developed by the Swiss typographer Hans Eduard Meier and originally published by the German typefoundry D. Stempel AG in 1969. It was their last new typeface cast in metal for letterpress printing. In the late 1990s, Syntax was revised by Meier himself and expanded into a superfamily.

Drawn as a counterpoint to the popular Grotesk-style Sans Serif typefaces produced in the 1950s, Syntax was based on Humanistic models. Syntax's letterforms are wide open. They have a tall x-height and very mild contrast. These properties ensure that the typeface is legible, especially in small sizes. Another peculiarity of Syntax is that it inclines slightly, which is unusual for a Sans Serif, but which gives the typeface a subtly-agile character. Syntax's terminals are at right angles to the strokes. This is particularly visible in the lower-case 'k' and 'x', making the typeface easy to recognise.

The properties described above – especially the tall x-height, open letterforms, and dynamic character – give Syntax its characteristic pattern in texts. The typeface is particularly suitable for use in body text. Syntax is supplemented by the other typefaces from its superfamily: Syntax Serif, Syntax Letter, and Syntax Lapidar.

Whenever the black fox jumped the squirrel gazed suspiciously.

Name	**Template Gothic**
Design	Barry Deck
Foundry	Emigre
Year	1991
Category	Display

Template Gothic was designed by the American type designer Barry Deck and published by Emigre in 1991.

Deck designed Template Gothic during his studies. He was inspired by a sign in a laundromat in his neighbourhood, which had been lettered with stencils. While many contemporary type designers were guided by the proportions of historical typefaces, Deck was more enthusiastic about imperfect everyday forms. He understood this kind of typeface as a reflection of peoples' imperfect everyday lives. Deck advocated for typography to go beyond traditional values like legibility.

Template Gothic is based on geometric stencil letterforms, and its stroke contrast varies greatly. Some stroke-endings are tapered, others are rounded. Some transitions are rounded, others have ink-traps. This irregularity is a feature of Template Gothic's special character.

With its concept of imperfection, Template Gothic was fully in line with the grunge style popular in typography, fashion, and music during the 1990s.

Whenever the black fox jumped the squirrel gazed suspiciously.

Name	Thesis Sans
Design	Luc(as) de Groot
Foundry	FontFont (Monotype)	Lucas Fonts
Year	1994
Category	(Dynamic) Sans Serif

TheSans was designed by Luc(as) de Groot as part of his Thesis superfamily. It was first published in 1994 by FontFont.

The comprehensive project aimed to create a coherent superfamily of well-developed typefaces that could all be combined. De Groot's super-family included a Sans Serif (TheSans), a Slab Serif (TheSerif), and a hybrid of both (TheMix). Each of those three variants has a variety of weights and companion italics, too. In due time, the families were expanded to include more widths. The fonts' character sets eventually grew to support Cyrillic and even Arabic.

Together with TheSerif, TheSans forms the core of the superfamily. Its letterforms have hardly any visible contrast. Their wide-open counters and relatively tall x-height – together with moderate ascenders and descenders – lead to the typefaces' good legibility.

With its extraordinary range of variants and styles, Thesis has gone down in history as a super-family pioneer.

Whenever the black fox jumped the squirrel gazed suspiciously.

Name	Thesis Serif
Design	Luc(as) de Groot
Foundry	FontFont (Monotype)	Lucas Fonts
Year	1994
Category	(Dynamic) Slab Serif

TheSerif was designed by Luc(as) de Groot as part of his Thesis superfamily. It was first published in 1994 by FontFont.

The comprehensive project aimed to create a coherent superfamily of well-developed typefaces that could all be combined. De Groot's super-family included a Sans Serif (TheSans), a Slab Serif (TheSerif), and a hybrid of both (TheMix). Each of those three variants has a variety of weights and companion italics, too. In due time, the families were expanded to include more widths. The fonts' character sets eventually grew to support Cyrillic and even Arabic.

Together with TheSans, TheSerif forms the core of the superfamily. Its letterforms have hardly any visible contrast. Their wide-open counters and relatively tall x-height – together with moderate ascenders and descenders – lead to the typefaces' good legibility. Serifs that are as thick as the letters' stems also contribute to TheSerif's robust yet friendly character.

Whenever the black fox jumped the squirrel gazed suspiciously.

T

Fonts A → Z

324

Name	ThreeSix
Design	Hamish Muir, Paul McNeil
Foundry	FontFont (Monotype)
Year	2011
Category	Display

FF ThreeSix was developed in 2011 by the British graphic designers Paul McNeil and Hamish Muir. It was published by FontFont.

It emerged out of an experiment its two designers undertook. They wanted to create typefaces inside a strict geometric grid. The result was an extensive typographic superfamily of eight variants, each with six weights, which were all based on a grid of 36 units. The typeface consists exclusively of straight lines and circular elements, with which arches and curves are constructed. In many letters, the arches are not closed – e.g., in the 'e', 'n', 'o', and 'u' – creating an interesting interplay of positive and negative.

The size and basic proportions of the letters remain the same, even in the different weights. This means that the heavier styles are particularly dark and the fine styles are very light and open in comparison. The omissions in the arches are very present there.

Due to its particularly reduced, strictly geometric construction, ThreeSix is most suited for head-lines and other display applications where a lot of character is needed.

Whenever the black fox jumped the squirrel gazed suspiciously.

Name	Times New Roman
Design	Stanley Morison, Victor Lardent
Foundry	Monotype
Year	1931
Category	(Dynamic) Serif

Times New Roman was designed by the British typographer Stanley Morison and the draughtsman Victor Lardent. It was published by the Monotype type-setting machine manufacturing company in 1931.

Times New Roman was commissioned by *The Times* newspaper after Stanley Morison had written an article critically addressing the news-paper's typography and printing. As a result, legibility under poor printing conditions, as well as a space-saving economy, were basic require-ments for the new typeface's design.

Its inspiration came primarily from the Monotype Plantin typeface, combined with influences from Transitional Serif typefaces. Times New Roman is characterised by its stroke contrast, tall x-height, and short ascenders and descenders. Letterforms were drawn relatively narrow so that they would save space. All of Times New Roman's features serve its legibility and provide for a high-quality image in print, even under poor conditions.

After a year of exclusive use by *The Times*, Times New Roman was released for Monotype to sell generally. It achieved great popularity around the world. It became even more widely-used later after it was added as a system font to Microsoft Windows and Apple's macOS. Thanks to its excellent readability and wide availability, it became one of the typefaces used most-often for body text setting.

Whenever the black fox jumped the squirrel gazed suspiciously.

Name	Tisa
Design	Mitja Miklavčič
Foundry	FontFont (Monotype)
Year	2008
Category	(Dynamic) Slab Serif

FF Tisa comes from the Slovenian type designer Mitja Miklavčič. The typeface was published by FontFont in 2008 and later served as the basis for the Tisa superfamily.

Formally inspired by Slab Serif wood type from the 19th century, Tisa was conceived as a contemporary typeface for use in magazine design. In contrast to its historical models, Tisa relies on Humanistic forms. The asymmetrical rounded tops of its slab serifs are also transferred to other areas of the letters that would usually be angular. In combination with the strong serifs, this creates a warm and friendly look. The contrast axis of Tisa's letterforms is slightly inclined and its counters are wide open, which ensures that text set in the typeface will be legible. Tisa's chamfered terminals emphasise its handwritten character.

Thanks to its dynamic, Humanistic features, Tisa is easy to read. After its publication, Tisa became popular not only in magazine design but also as a webfont. The typeface works well in body text, and generally in all areas of visual communication, too. Tisa was later joined by a Sans Serif companion called Tisa Sans.

Whenever the black fox jumped the squirrel gazed suspiciously.

Name	**Tisa Sans**
Design	Mitja Miklavčič
Foundry	FontFont (Monotype)
Year	2008
Category	(Dynamic) Sans Serif

FF Tisa Sans comes from the Slovenian type designer Mitja Miklavčič. It was published by Font-Font in 2008 and is part of the Tisa superfamily.

Formally inspired by Slab Serif wood type from the 19th century, Tisa was conceived as a contemporary typeface for use in magazine design. Tisa Sans is a Sans Serif version that was developed from Tisa.

Generally speaking, Tisa Sans's letterforms come from Tisa. Its letters are wide open and the terminals are rounded off. Stroke endings are even a little more round than in Tisa itself and this creates a brush-like character, especially in Tisa Sans' heavier weights.

Thanks to its dynamic, Humanistic features, Tisa Sans is easy to read and is very popular in corporate communication, as well as in the design of navigation systems. The typeface is an extension of a Slab Serif design named Tisa.

Yoann

THE QUICK BROWN FOX JUMPS OVER THE LAZY DOG.

Name	**Trajan**
Design	Carol Twombly
Foundry	Adobe
Year	(113)	1989
Category	Display

Trajan was developed by the American type designer Carol Twombly as part of the Adobe Originals programme in 1989.

Trajan is an interpretation of stone-carved inscriptional letters in the Capitalis Monumentalis style on the base of the Trajan Column in Rome, from 113 A.D. The Trajan typeface is not the first typographic interpretation of the inscription. But because of its number of weights and styles – and because the family is distributed by Adobe – it is the most well-known.

Like its historical model, Trajan only has capital letters, but the fonts have small caps in them, and the family has a bold style, too. The typeface is especially characterised by its moderate contrast and fine, bracketed serifs. Another characteristic feature is the long swash-like tail of the 'Q'.

With its very classical, Roman character – and because it only has capital letters – Trajan is only suitable for short texts. It can be used in headlines as well as in other display applications. The typeface has been particularly well-received thanks to the epic feeling it lends to film poster designs and book covers.

Whenever the black fox jumped the squirrel gazed suspiciously.

Name	**Unger Fraktur**
Design	Johann Friedrich Unger (1793), Ralph M. Unger (2010)
Foundry	Unger | Linotype (Monotype)
Year	1793 | 2010
Category	Blackletter (Fraktur)

The Unger Fraktur typeface was cut by the Berlin printer and typographer Johann Friedrich Unger in 1793. A digital interpretation of Unger's design was developed by the German type designer Ralph M. Unger for Monotype in 2010.

The Unger Fraktur arose from the desire to modernise the forms of Fraktur and to create a rational Blackletter typeface with international appeal. With this aim in mind, Unger tried to transfer the stylistic elements and design parameters of Static Serif typefaces like Bodoni or Didot – which were popular at that time – to a Fraktur typeface. In the design process, Unger worked closely together with Firmin Didot, who cut the first three trials for the typeface. The final version was cut by Unger with the help of his assistant Johann Christoph Gubitz. The Unger Fraktur has the brightness and clarity of Static Serif types, thanks to its generous counters. The usual flourishes and ornaments from Fraktur designs are strongly reduced. The filigree curved elements, in contrast to the geometrically constructed forms, indicate Didot's influence. Above all, the Unger Fraktur is characterised by its lower-case 'm', 'n', and 'u': the arches of those letters are abstracted into straight lines, the stems end in diamond-shaped terminals.

The Unger Fraktur did not achieve much popularity when it was published. At the beginning of the 20th century, a few fonts of the typeface were found in the Enschedé printing house in Haarlem. After that point, it did become commercially successful and experienced wider distribution.

Robert

Whenever the black fox jumped the squirrel gazed suspiciously.

Name	**Univers**
Design	Adrian Frutiger
Foundry	Deberny & Peignot (Monotype)
Year	1957
Category	(Static) Sans Serif

Univers was developed by the Swiss type designer Adrian Frutiger and published by the Parisian typefoundry Deberny & Peignot in 1957.

The basis for Univers – as well as for Helvetica, which was published in the same year – was the archetypical Sans Serif forms in Akzidenz Grotesk. The different styles of the Univers family were drawn by Frutiger as part of a consistent system. This originally included two slopes, four widths, and six weights, resulting in 21 type styles whose formal relationships are illustrated in their names. Those style names were simply a combination of two numbers (e. g., Univers 57 for the family's regular weight, in a condensed width). The system was published as a clear matrix along with all the fonts themselves.

Univers stands out from other Sans Serif typefaces through its less-geometric letterforms.
Univers is mainly characterised by its tall x-height and moderate ascenders and descenders. Its letterforms are closed and exhibit hardly any stroke contrast. Its terminals are all either vertical or horizontal, which creates a decisive, clear overall impression.

Together with Helvetica, Univers stands for the Sans Serif typefaces of the 1950s and 1960s.
It is one of the typefaces used most often today.

Whenever the black fox jumped the squirrel gazed suspiciously.

Name	Verdana
Design	Matthew Carter
Foundry	Microsoft
Year	1996
Category	(Dynamic) Sans Serif

Verdana was made by the British type designer Matthew Carter for Microsoft in 1996.

As commissioned work for Microsoft, Carter intended for Verdana to be a scalable font for use on-screen, which would be easy to read even on monitors with poor resolution. In contrast to other screen fonts used at that time – which either had a fixed size or were developed first for large sizes and then scaled down – Carter developed Verdana in small sizes for the screen first. Only afterwards did he scale it up and draw the outlines needed for the font to work in print.

These technical requirements and its particular design process gave Verdana its characteristic pattern in text, with its tall x-height, open letters, and straight terminals. Together with Tom Rickner, the fonts were optimised in detail for various display sizes and on-screen use. Subsequently, Verdana was implemented in Microsoft Windows and was quickly distributed worldwide as a system font. In the meantime, it can be found on every Windows and Apple computer as a pre-installed font.

In 2011, Verdana was released in a new version as an OpenType font with a number of new styles and OpenType features, like ligatures and small caps. Today, it is still one of the most-used fonts.

Whenever the black fox jumped the squirrel gazed suspiciously.

Name	Zapf Chancery
Design	Hermann Zapf
Foundry	ITC
Year	1979
Category	Handwritten (Script)

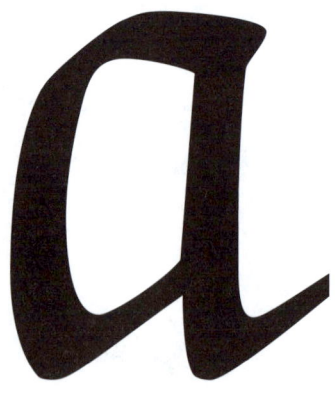

Zapf Chancery was designed by the German typographer and type designer Hermann Zapf for the International Typeface Corporation (ITC) in 1979.

The typeface was shaped by Zapf's many years of work as a calligrapher. It is formally based on Italian chancery handwriting styles from the High Renaissance. This handwritten origin is revealed in the letters' slant – which is visible even in the upright (or 'roman' style) – as well as in the form of its strokes. Zapf Chancery is easy to read thanks to the clear design of its letterforms. The typeface's strongly swashed ascenders and descenders, as well as the swash-formed ornamented capitals, are very recognisable.

Zapf Chancery became particularly popular due to its implementation in Apple computers from the mid-1980s and the subsequent boom in Desktop Publishing.

Zapf Chancery is suitable for applications where an emphatically-calligraphic character should be expressed.

Simon

Serif

Arnhem 2002

Whenever the black fox jum

Athelas 2008

Whenever the black fox jum

Baskerville 1757 | 1978

Whenever the black fox jum

Beirut Display 2014

Whenever the black fox jum

Beirut Text 2014

Whenever the black fox jump

Bely 2016

Whenever the black fox jum

Whenever the black fox ju

Whenever the black fox ju

Whenever the black fox ju

Whenever the black fox ju

Whenever the black fox ju

Whenever the black fox ju

Whenever the black fox ju

Whenever the black fox ju

Fedra Serif 2003

Whenever the black fox jump

Filosofia 1996

Whenever the black fox jump

Garamond 1538 | 1989

Whenever the black fox jump

Georgia 1996

Whenever the black fox jum

IBM Plex Serif 2017

Whenever the black fox jum

Jenson 1470 | 1996

Whenever the black fox jump

Karloff Positive 2012

Whenever the black fox jumpe

Minion 1989

Whenever the black fox jum

Mrs Eaves [1996]

Whenever the black fox ju

Noe Display [2013]

Whenever the black fox ju

Noe Text [2015]

Whenever the black fox ju

Pensum [2016]

Whenever the black fox ju

Rotis Serif [1988]

Whenever the black fox ju

Sabon [1964]

Whenever the black fox ju

SangBleu Empire [2017]

Whenever the black fox ju

Scala [1991]

Whenever the black fox ju

Sectra [2013]

Whenever the black fox jum

Spectral [2017]

Whenever the black fox jum

Swift [1987 | 2009]

Whenever the black fox jum

Times New Roman [1931]

Whenever the black fox jum

Slab Serif

Adelle [2009]

Whenever the black fox jum

American Typewriter [1974]

Whenever the black fox jump

Caecilia [1991]

Whenever the black fox jump

Clarendon [1845 | 1951]

Whenever the black fox ju

Courier [1955]

The quick brown fox

Karloff Negative [2012]

Whenever the black fox jun

Karloff Neutral [2012]

Whenever the black fox ju

Nordvest [2016]

Whenever the black fox ju

Rockwell [1934]

Whenever the black fox ju

Thesis Serif [1994]

Whenever the black fox ju

Tisa [2008]

Whenever the black fox ju

Sans Serif

Akkurat 2004

Whenever the black fox jump

Akzidenz Grotesk 1898 | 1958

Whenever the black fox jumpe

Antique Olive 1962

Whenever the black fox jumpe

Avant Garde 1970

Whenever the black fox jump

Avenir 1988

Whenever the black fox jum

Bell Centennial 1976

Whenever the black fox jumpe

Brown 2011

Whenever the black fox jum

Cargo [2003]

Whenever the black fox jum

Circular [2013]

Whenever the black fox ju

Clan [2006–2008]

Whenever the black fox jum

Darby Sans Poster [2014]

Whenever the black fox jur

DIN [1931 | 1995]

Whenever the black fox jur

Favorit [2016]

Whenever the black fox ju

Fedra Sans [2001]

Whenever the black fox jun

Franklin Gothic [1902 | 1980]

Whenever the black fox jun

Frutiger 1975 | 2000

Whenever the black fox jumpe

Futura 1927 | 2013

Whenever the black fox jum

Gill Sans 1927

Whenever the black fox jum

Gotham 2000

Whenever the black fox jum

Greta Sans 2012

Whenever the black fox jump

Gräbenbach 2016

Whenever the black fox jumpe

Haptik 2014

Whenever the black fox jum

Helvetica 1957

Whenever the black fox jumpe

IBM Plex Mono [2017]

The quick brown fox

IBM Plex Sans [2017]

Whenever the black fox jun

Infini [2015]

Whenever the black fox ju

International [2014]

Whenever the black fox ju

Interstate [1993]

Whenever the black fox ju

Letter Gothic [1962 | 1989]

The quick brown fox j

Meta [1991]

Whenever the black fox jun

National [2007]

Whenever the black fox ju

News Gothic [1908]

Whenever the black fox jumped th

Nitti [2008]

The quick brown fox :

Noto Sans [2013]

Whenever the black fox jump

Optima [1958]

Whenever the black fox jum

Ping [2019]

Whenever the black fox jump

Replica [2008]

Whenever the black fox jump

Rotis Sans Serif [1988]

Whenever the black fox jumped

SangBleu Sunrise [2017]

Whenever the black fox jum

Scala Sans [1994]

Whenever the black fox ju

Simple [2002]

The quick brown fox ju

Syntax [1969 | 2000]

Whenever the black fox jur

Thesis Sans [1994]

Whenever the black fox jur

Tisa Sans [2008]

Whenever the black fox ju

Univers [1957]

Whenever the black fox ju

Verdana [1996]

Whenever the black fox ju

Display

Amelia [1966]

Whenever the fox jumpe

Architype Stedelijk [1968 | 1997]

whenever the black fox jumped the

Bauhaus [1925 | 1975]

Whenever the black fox jump

Blur [1991]

Whenever the black fox jum

Clifton [2014–2017]

Whenever the squi

Cooper Black [1922]

Whenever the fox jumpe

Dot Matrix [1991–1998]

The quick brown fox jun

FE-Mittelschrift 1980 | 1997

WHENEVER THE FOX JUMPE

Kada 2002

THE QUICK BROWN FOX

Lo-Res 1985 | 2001

The quick brown fox ju

Lÿno Jean 2010

THE QUICK BROWN FOX JU

Minérale 2018

Whenever the black fox ju

Minuscule 2005

The quick br■wn f■x

New Alphabet 1967 | 1997

Whenever the black fox ju

Orientation 2018

The quick brown fox ju

Pareto [2016]

The quick brown fox jump

Template Gothic [1991]

Whenever the black fox jump

ThreeSix [2011]

Whenever the black fox jump

Trajan (113) | 1989

THE QUICK BROWN FOX J

Handwritten

Bello Script [2004]

Whenever the black fox jumped

Brush Script [1942]

Whenever the black fox jump

Comic Sans [1995]

Whenever the black fox jum

Mistral [1953]

Whenever the black fox jum

Zapf Chancery [1979]

Whenever the black fox jump

Blackletter

Alte Schwabacher [1470 | 1992]

Whenever the black fox jum

Brokenscript [1991]

Whenever the black fox ju

Eskapade Fraktur [2012]

Whenever the black fox jum

Fakir [2006]

Whenever the fox jum

Fette Fraktur [1873 | 1993]

Whenever the black fox jum

Harbour 1998

The quick brown fox ju

Lucida Blackletter 1991

Whenever the black fox jumpe

Old English 1901 | 2001

Whenever the black fox jump

San Marco 1991

Whenever the black fox jumpe

Unger Fraktur 1793 | 2010

Whenever the black fox jumpe

Glossary

Principles of Form

The **Formal Principle** is the basic principle of design underlying the character of a typeface. The Formal Principle influences a typeface's impact and legibility. Among other things, it has consequences for a typeface's orientation and the contrast axis, as well as the shape and proportions of the letters.

Dynamic Principle of Form

Typefaces with a Dynamic Principle of Form are formally related to letterforms that were written with a broad pen (the principle of translation or modulating strokes). They have a diagonal contrast axis and their in-strokes are usually diagonal as well. The letterforms are differentiated from one another and open ('a', 'c', 'e', and 's'). The capitals are based on proportions from the Ancient Roman Capitalis Monumentalis.

Dynamic Principle of Form

Static Principle of Form

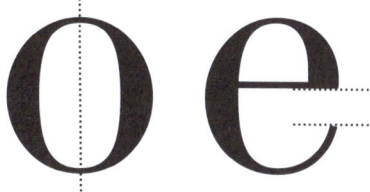

Geometric Principle of Form

Static Principle of Form

Typefaces with a Static (rational) Principle of Form are related to letterforms that are written with a pointed pen (the principle of expansion or swelling strokes). They have a vertical contrast axis and their in-strokes are usually horizontal. The letterforms seem to have a symmetrical construction and are closed ('a', 'c', 'e', and 's'). The proportions of the capital letters have been equalised, and all capitals have approximately the same width.

Geometric Principle of Form

Typefaces based on the Geometric Principle of Form look constructed. Their texture is determined by straight lines and curved circle-segments.

Informal

There are also type-faces that are not constructed according to the Dynamic, Static or Geometric Principles of Form.

Sandrine

Verena

Roxane

Character Style

Geometric
The letters of geometric typefaces are constructed out of basic geometric shapes (triangles, circles, and squares).

Italic
The term italic describes a type style whose letterforms slopes to the right. This type style is usually drawn as a companion to its respective upright typeface. 'true italic' styles have their own letterforms with roots reflecting different formal developments. Strictly speaking, when a font is automatically obliqued (or slanted) by a computer, it is not usually considered to be a 'true italic' typeface.

Modular
Modular typefaces are characterised by their being constructed out of a limited number of basic shapes (or modules).

Monolinear
Monolinear typefaces have no (or almost no) stroke contrast. Therefore, the glyphs have the same optical stroke thickness all over.

Monospace
Monospace typefaces are non-proportional. Each letter has the same width. Originally, these typefaces were used on typewriters. Because of their proportions, monospace typefaces are not suitable for long passages of text.

Geometric → Futura

Roger

Italic → Temeraire Italienne

Monolinear → Letter Gothic

Lucas

Monospace → IBM Plex Mono

Tobias

Oblique
Visually, the oblique type style is the result of an upright typeface whose letters have been slanted. This slanting (or obliquing) describes an automatic skewing process in which a computer deforms the typeface. Oblique typefaces should be differentiated from 'true italic' styles, which have a unique kind of letterform construction.

Proportional
A proportional typeface is a typeface where individual letters have their own widths. The opposite of a proportional typeface is a monospace type-face; the letters in those are non-proportional.

Rotated
In rotated typefaces, all the glyphs are rotated at the same specific angle.

Rounded
Rounded typefaces are characterised by their rounded stroke endings.

Underlined
Underlined type is used in typography to call attention to something, similar to the way one might italicise a word or other short part of a text. There are type-faces and type styles in which the underlines are already part of the glyphs.

Unicase
Unicase typefaces feature letters that are a hybrid between upper-case and lower-case. Some of the letterforms in a unicase alphabet might look like upper-case letters,

Akiem

Fiona

Carol

Sibylle

Contrast Axis → Jenson

Roger

Reverse Contrast → Nordvest

Roxane

High Stroke Contrast → Didot

Low Stroke Contrast → Ping

Bram

others like lower-case ones, but they all share a common height.

Contrast

Contrast Axis
In typefaces with stroke contrast, the stroke thickness changes around a contrast axis. The contrast axis runs through the parts of a letter that have the least stroke thickness. In terms of inclination, the contrast axis can be completely vertical, or it can be slightly or strongly diagonal.

Reverse Contrast
With reverse contrast, the conventional distribution of the thick and thin strokes inside the letters is switched around: in this situation, the vertical strokes are thin and the horizontal strokes and serifs (if present) are thick.

Stroke Contrast
The stroke contrast (also referred to simply as contrast, or stroke-thickness contrast) describes the difference between a typeface's thick and thin strokes. This contrast is an essential feature for differentiating typefaces. For Static Serif typefaces like Didot, stroke contrast is very high.

General Terms

Capitalis Monumentalis

The Capitalis Monumentalis was the style of inscriptional letterforms used on monuments in the Roman Empire. It only has majuscule letters. The proportions of the letterforms are based on the square or are derived from squares. The letters were drawn onto a stone with a wide brush and then carved, which is why this style is also called Lapidary (from the Latin *lapis*, for 'stone').

Carolingian Minuscule

The Carolingian minuscule is a handwriting style once used for book text. It was developed during the second half of the 8th century and is characterised by a clear and simple appearance. Under Charlemagne's rule, it quickly spread from the Carolingian Empire's writing centres (including Aachen, Tours, and Reims) to places across Europe. The letters from the Gothic minuscule – and the later Humanistic minuscule that emerged out of it – were ultimately the predecessors of the Latin script's lower-case.

Character

An element in a typeface's character set is called a character. For example, this can be a letter, a ligature or a punctuation mark. The visual representation of a character is called a glyph.

Gothic Minuscule
The Gothic minuscule is a handwriting style once used for book text. It was developed in scriptoria during the Gothic period in the Middle Ages. It emerged in the 12th century, replacing the Carolingian minuscule. Around 1300, it influenced the development of a later book hand: Textura.

Humanistic Minuscule
The Humanistic minuscule is a handwriting style once used for book text. It developed out of the Carolingian minuscule and emerged in Florence and Padua at the beginning of the 15th century. The lower-case letters for the Latin script grew out of this style.

Script
The term 'script' describes a system of characters that represent language visually.

Texture
Texture refers to the visual appearance of the characters in a typeface and the overall impression they give in a text. Various factors influence texture, including the proportions of letters and their stroke thickness. Typefaces can be distinguished from one another by their textures, too.

Type Classification
Type classification refers to the division of typefaces into typeface categories and subcategories. A typeface's various character properties can be useful in classification. There are different classification approaches.

For instance, typefaces can be grouped according to chronological or formal aspects. Common classification systems for Latin-script typefaces include British Standards 2961, DIN 16518, and Vox-ATypI.

Type Family

Type family is the term for a typeface, including all various font styles that may be associated with it.

Type Size

Type size is denoted in points. The relative dimensions of cap-heights, x-heights, ascenders, and descenders can differ significantly between two typefaces, even at the same type size. Therefore, a typeface's overall effect in text is dependent on the sizes of these elements, in addition to other factors.

Type Style

The different stylistic variants within a type family are called type styles. Distinctions are made according to weight (normal, bold, etc.), optical size (titling, text, etc.), width (condensed, extended, etc.), and slant (normal, italic, oblique).

Type Width

Type width refers to the relative amount of horizontal space a typeface takes up. It has a direct influence on the amount of space a typeface uses on a line.

Typeface

A typeface is a specific design of type that can be identified by name. Colloquially, 'font' is also used.

Typeface Category

Typefaces with similar design features can be assigned to groups. Common type classification systems like British Standards 2961, DIN 16518, or Vox-ATypI organise typefaces into multiple typeface categories, classes, or groups.

Typeface Slant

The typeface slant designates a type style's angle or slope. One distinguishes between upright, oblique, and italic type styles.

Writing System

A writing system is a set of symbols that represent language. There are different writing systems, e.g., Arabic, Chinese, Cyrillic, Hangul, Hebrew, Latin, etc.

Letterform Anatomy

Aperture

The term aperture describes the distance between two strokes in a character that do not enclose an interior form (e.g., in 'a', 'c', 'e', or 's'). The size of the characters' apertures influences a typeface's legibility. Characters with a small aperture are described as being closed, those with a wide aperture are referred to as open.

Ascender

The ascender is the part of a lower-case letter that extends upward from the x-height.

Baseline

The baseline is a horizontal guideline on which a typeface's characters stand. The x-height, cap-height, ascenders, descenders, and line-height are all measured from the baseline. For optical compensation, the parts of letterforms that are round or pointed can extend slightly below the baseline, just as they can overshoot the x-height or cap-height, too, etc.

Bowl

The round part of a letter, which surrounds a counter, is called a bowl.

Bracketing

Bracketing refers to the usually round-shaped transitions connecting serifs with a stem. The degree of bracketing can vary, in terms of how pronounced it looks.

Ascender / Descender → American Typewriter

Sibylle

Baseline → Orientation

Bram

Cap-Height → Minérale

Verena

Counter → IBM Plex Mono

Tobias

Cap-Height

The cap-height refers to the height of the capitals (upper-case letters) relative to the baseline.

Capital

This is a term for an upper-case letter of an alphabet (also called a majuscule).

Counter

The non-printing inside shapes of a letter (the so-called 'interior form') is a counter. Counters can be open ('c') or closed ('o').

Descender

The descender is the part of a lower-case letter that extends downward from the baseline.

Down-Stroke

This term comes from calligraphy. The down-stroke refers to a part of a letter that – when written with a broad pen – is thick. In contrast to this, an up-stroke is a fine line made when the broad pen moves upward from the bottom-left to the top-right.

Ductus

The term ductus refers to the characteristic forms of a typeface that were originally derived from the writing tool: e.g., stroke thickness, stroke inclination, and the stroke pattern of the characters.

Foot

The foot is the lower area of a stroke terminal or leg standing on the baseline.

Hairline
The thin stroke of a character, in contrast to the wider stroke called a stem, is called a hairline.

In-Stroke
The in-stroke is a term for a stroke's upper part, or wherever a stroke begins. When the in-stroke is diagonally shaped, it suggests the kinds of forms written with a broad pen. When the in-stroke is horizontal, it is reminiscent of a stroke that could be made with a pointed pen.

Interior Form
The interior form (or interior space) of the non-printing counter shape inside of a letter. Interior forms can be open ('c') or closed ('o').

Leg
A diagonal down-stroke, like those found on the 'K' or the 'R', is called a leg.

Ligature
A ligature is a connection between two (or more) letters.

Loop
The lower bowl of a double-storey (double-bowled) 'g' is called a loop.

Lower-Case
The term for the small letters of the alphabet (i.e., the letters that are not called 'capitals' or 'upper-case'). Also referred to with the term 'minuscule'.

Majuscule
A term for the capital letters of an alphabet (also called upper-case letters).

In-Stroke → Beirut Text

Sibylle

Out-Stroke → Georgia

Zuzana

Lower-Case → Beowolf

Fiona

Stem → Gotham

Tobias

Mean-Height

The mean-height, usually called the x-height, is a term describing the height of a typeface's lower-case letters without ascenders and descenders.

Minuscule

A term for the small letters of an alphabet (also called lower-case letters).

Neck

The vertical stroke on the right-hand side of the letter 'G' is called the neck (or shaft).

Out-Stroke

As a term, the out-stroke (and also the terminal, or stroke terminal) refers to the design of the end of a stroke that is part of a letterform. Some out-strokes end in clearly-formed terminals.

These terminals can take various shapes. For instance, the terminal at the top of a lowercase 'a' or at the bottom of the lower-case 'y' might be a round object. In that case, it is referred to as a 'ball terminal.'

Serifs

Serifs (also sometimes called 'feet') are the concluding horizontal flicks at the end of a typeface's strokes. One distinguishes between head serifs and foot serifs. The word 'serif' probably comes from the Dutch *schreef*, for stroke or line. The Capitalis Monumentalis or the Capitalis Quadrata are generally considered to be the origin of the serif itself. It is assumed that serifs developed less from a technical need and more because of formal aesthetic reasons. Serifs can be divided into three groups based on their general form and stroke thickness: serifs that are as thick as the typeface's hair-lines, serifs as thick as the typeface's stems, and tapering 'wedge-shaped' serifs. Further-more, serifs can differ in terms of how they transition from a typeface's stems. Moderate transitions feature a smooth curve connecting the stem and the serif (one also speaks of bracketed serifs here). Sudden transitions are charac-terised an abrupt or an-gled transition between the stem and the serif.

Small Caps
Small caps are smaller-sized capital letters that are drawn at the approximate height of the lower-case letters.

Spur
The spur is a small out-growth at the end of a stem. It creates optical compensation at the junctions of a stem and curve (such as in 'b', 'G', and 'q').

Stem
The vertical, straight, and – at the same time – thickest stroke of a letter is called a stem (also a shaft or a main stroke).

Storey
The lower-case 'a' and 'g' come in two different basic forms. The single-storey 'a' has one interior form, while the double- storey 'a' has two separate interior forms. The single-storey (single-bowled) 'g' and the double-storey (double-bowled) 'g' also have the same relation-ship.

Stroke Thickness
The stroke thickness (or line width) denotes the thickness of a character's stem. The different weights (type styles) within a typeface family will each feature a different stroke thickness: e.g., stroke thickness will get thicker from thin, light, normal, medium, bold, black, etc. Typefaces can have an optically mono-linear stroke thickness or more-or-less visible differences in stroke thickness.

Tail
The tail is an out-stroke that sweeps outward (such as on the 'Q' or 'R').

x-Height
The x-height, also called the mean-height, describes the height of a typeface's lower-case letters, without ascenders and descenders. It is measured by the height of the lower-case x. A tall x-height can foster the legibility of a typeface.

Materiality

Broad Pen
Writing with a broad pen creates stroke-contrast that almost always is caused by the direction of the stroke movement. The contrast axis tends to incline to the left. In particular, a broad-pen ductus can be observed in Dynamic Serif typefaces, which were first developed under the influence of Humanistic hand-writing styles during the Renaissance.

Dot Matrix
Typefaces based on a dot matrix are made up from dots on a grid. They are often used on LED display boards.

Inscription
An inscription is a short text that is either attached to the material bearing it or embedded into that material itself. The letterforms used for inscriptions usually have writing-tool characteristics (such as those that could easily be cut with a hammer and chisel).

Pixel Typeface
A pixel typeface (bitmap font) is a typeface whose letters are made up out of square pixels. These typefaces were originally used to render text on computer screens. For each point size, there was a separate font.

Carol

BRAM

Kris

Emilie

Pointed Pen

Writing with a pointed pen allows for the stroke thickness to change at any particular point through the application or reduction of pressure to the nib. In particular, a pointed-pen ductus can be observed in typography thanks to Static Serif typefaces, which were first developed under the influence of rationally-constructed letter-forms during the Neo-classical era.

Stencil Typeface

Stencil typefaces are characterised by the bridges inter-rupting their letters. This feature references the mechanics of making lettering with metal stencils.

Typewriter

Typefaces that were originally designed for the typewriter are characterised by their proportions. For mechanical reasons, all characters have the same width. These typefaces are also called non-proportional typefaces or monospace typefaces. Their counterparts are proportional typefaces, in which each character has a unique width of its own.

Note: These are just a few examples of visual reminiscences of materiality in typefaces.

Technology

OpenType

OpenType is a font file format based on the earlier TrueType format. It allows for characters to be encoded with Unicode. The OpenType format is cross-platform. Through the use of so-called OpenType features, it allows for specific typographic refinements to be portrayed (such as ligatures, alternate glyphs, etc). In 2016, OpenType 1.8 introduced support for variable fonts.

Screen Typeface

Screen typefaces are developed for use on a monitor.

SIL OFL

The SIL Open Font License was issued by the Summer Institute of Linguistics. Fonts with this specification are recognised as libre software products and can be used for free. They are classified along with other open source fonts.

Variable Font

Variable fonts are interpolatable OpenType fonts. With the help of various axes (weight, width, slant, etc.), different font styles can be generated.

Note: These are just a few exemples of technology in typefaces.

Usage

Body Text
A longer passage of text set at a reading size of e. g., 10 to 12 point is referred to by the term body text.

Headline Typeface
Headline typefaces (also called Display or titling typefaces) are typefaces that are suitable for use in large type sizes. They can be used to highlight a title or a short text, especially in reading sizes from 14 to 48 points. Some typeface families include special 'display' styles, which have been optically adjusted to be different from the family's respective text styles in terms of stroke contrast and proportion. For display sizes above 48 points, headline typefaces can also be used when reading will take place at a greater distance.

Multi-Script Typeface
The character sets in multi-script typefaces contain glyphs for more than one writing system at a time. In addition to the Latin script, the other scripts in a multi-script typeface could include Arabic, Chinese, Cyrillic, Hangul, Hebrew, etc.

Newspaper Typeface
Newspaper typefaces are text typefaces that were originally optimised for use in newspapers; however, they can be used in other ways for longer texts intended for immersive reading, too. To support the leading of the eye across a line of text, Serif typefaces are typically used

– particularly typefaces with strong serifs. Other common features of newspaper typefaces are a tall x-height and narrow letter proportions.

Printing Types
This term comes from the letterpress-printing era, when printed works were assembled from individual pieces of movable metal type – one for each character. Printing types were how one referred to fonts of metal type that would be used in text composition and printing.

Small Text Sizes
Some typefaces or type styles were designed especially for small type sizes. These are used for captions, usually in sizes from 6 to 8 point. They have optical adjustments like low stroke contrast and tall x-heights. Further adjustments, such as ink traps, can lead to peculiar letterform designs.

Super Family
A super family is a collection of typefaces designed as a unit, but whose representatives can be assigned to different typeface categories. All typefaces in a super family usually have the same basic forms and proportions, which is why they tend to harmonise well with each other optically.

Text Typeface
Typefaces that are particularly suitable for longer passages of text are called text typefaces. Their use is especially common for texts set at reading sizes from 10 to 12 point.

www.typ-o.eu
check it out!

Index

The conception, design and editorial work of the app were carried out by the 'typ/o' project team from the department of design at the FH Aachen, under the direction of Prof. Eva Kubinyi and Robin Coenen. The student assistants were Marco Bazelmans, Andreas Blindert, Uli Holtschlag, Robert Franke, Lara Liske, Henry Monse, Paul Theisen, and Simon Thiefes.

The project 'www.typ-o.eu' was funded by the 'Fellowship für Innovation in der digitalen Hochschullehre 2019' of the Ministry of Innovation, Science and Research of the state of North Rhine-Westphalia and the Stifterverband.

Check out the app: www.typ-o.eu

The 'typ/o' project was conceived as a free educational mobile-first website for recognising and classifying typefaces.

Its goal is not to automatically identify individual fonts, but to facilitate the learning of how to recognise their underlying formal principles.

As a basis, various terms and group divisions in current international use have been relied on here. This means that slight deviations from existing norms for classifying typefaces have consciously been made.

In particular, 'typ/o' can be used in the classroom for motivating students and fostering curiosity about investigating typography.

In the 'Learn' section, basic information about how typefaces are grouped into categories and subcategories is presented. That is supplemented with historical information and explanations of formal particularities.

The most important technical terms are also explained in the 'Glossary'.

In the 'Identify' section, users can compare typefaces found in everyday life (e.g., in the cityscape), or that they encounter in their studies, with the models shown. The correct classification depends on the precision of the identification path. As a didactic exercise, the typeface to be determined (photo) can be compared with the result (screenshot) in class.

In the 'Play' section, users can check what they have learned playfully. The 'Fonts' catalogue has a selection of more than 100 typefaces, with relevant background information. These typefaces can be filtered and displayed according to specific criteria (such as by category, the formal principle, favourites, etc).

All typefaces are classified according to their respective regular-style font.

www.typ-o.eu

Index of Typefaces

Index of Technical Terms

Index of Foundries

Our thanks go out to the numerous foundries and designers who supported us by providing the fonts shown here. The copyright and licensing rights for the typefaces shown are held by their respective foundries.

This publication and the website are composed with Infini, a typeface designed by Sandrine Nugue for CNAP. → www.cnap.fr

Attempts have been made to locate the sources of all images and licence-holders to obtain full reproduction rights, but in the very few cases where this process has failed to find the copyright holder, our apologies are offered.

Bibliography

Phil Baines, Andrew Haslam, *Type & Typography*, Laurence King Publishing 2002

Lewis Blackwell, *Twentieth-Century Type*, Bangert Verlag, München 1992

Max Bollwage, *Buchstaben-geschichte(n): wie das Alphabet entstand und warum unsere Buch-staben so aussehen*, Akademische Druck- und Verlagsanstalt, Graz 2010

Robert Bringhurst, *The elements of typographic style*, Hartley & Marks, Seattle 2005

Karen Cheng, *Anatomie der Buchstaben – Basiswissen für Schriftgestalter*, Hermann Schmidt Mainz 2006

Taylor Childers, Jessica Griscti, Liberty Leben, *25 Systems for Classifying Typography: A Study in Naming Frequency*, In: *Parsons Journal for Information Mapping*, New York 2013

Stephen Coles, *The Anatomy of Type: A Graphic Guide to 100 Typefaces*, Harper Design, New York 2012

Peter Dawson, *The Field Guide to Typography: Typefaces in the Urban Landscape*, Prestel 2013

Catherine Dixon, *Typeface classification*, A talk given at the conference *Twentieth century graphic communication; technology, society & culture* held by *The Friends of St Bride Printing Library*, 24–25 September 2002, London (script)

Damien Gautier, Claire Gautier, *Gestaltung, Typografie etc.: Ein Handbuch*, Niggli Verlag 2010

Gutenberg Museum, *Neue Schriften. New typefaces*, Niggli Verlag 2013

Andres Janser, Christina Reble, *Frische Schriften. Fresh Type*, Edition Museum für Gestaltung Zürich 2004

Stephanie und Ralf de Jong, *Schriftwechsel*, Hermann Schmidt Mainz 2008

Eva Kubinyi, *Typeface? Classification*, In: *Yearbook of type 2021/22*, Slanted Publishers 2021

Eva Kubinyi, Robin Coenen, *Typ/o, an educational app for typeface classification*, ATypI 2020 (talk)

Indra Kupferschmid, *Buchstaben kommen selten allein – Ein typografisches Handbuch*, Niggli Verlag 2003

Indra Kupferschmid, *Can AI help classify and select typefaces?*, In: *Back Office #2*, Éditions B42 2018

Indra Kupferschmid, *Some type genres explained*, 2016, www.kupferschrift.de

Indra Kupferschmid, *Type classifications are useful, but the common ones are not*, 2012, www.kupferschrift.de

Samuel Marty, Richard Frick, *Der Schriftenfächer: Eine Entdeckungsreise*, Züricher Hochschule der Künste (ZHdK) und Berufsschule für Gestaltung Zürich (BfGZ) 2016

Paul McNeil, *Visual History of Type*, Laurence King Publishing 2017

Gerrit Noordzij, *Broken Scripts and the Classification of Typefaces*, In: *The Journal of Typographic Research Volume IV, Number 3*, Summer 1970

Gerrit Noordzij, *The Stroke – theory of writing*, Hyphen Press, London 2005

Sandrine Nugue, *Specimen Infini*, CNAP Paris 2014

Jörg Petri, *Klassenlose Schrift. Schriftklassifikationen im Wandel analoger und digitaler Typografie*, Kassel University Press 2020

Joep Pohlen, *Letterfontäne: Die Anatomie der Schrift*, Taschen Verlag Köln 2011

René Ponot, *Classification typographique*, In: *Communication et langage n°81*, 3e trimestre 1989

Sauthoff, Wendt, Willberg, *Schriften erkennen*, Hermann Schmidt Mainz 1996

Erich Schulz-Anker,
*Formanalyse und Dokumentation
einer serifenlosen Linearschrift
auf neuer Basis: Syntax-Antiqua,*
D. Stempel AG, Frankfurt 1969

Tony Seddon, *The Evolution
of Type,* Thames & Hudson 2015

*The Phaidon Archive of Graphic
Design,* Phaidon Press 2012

Francis Thibaudeau,
*Manuel français de Typographie
moderne,* bureau de l'édition,
Paris 1924

Jan Tschichold, *Eine
neue Klassifizierung der Buch-
druckschriften,* 1951;
In: Jan Tschichold, *Schriften:
1925–1974,* Brinkmann und
Bose, Berlin 1992

Hans Peter Willberg,
Wegweiser Schrift, Hermann
Schmidt Mainz 2001

Michael Wörgötter, *TypeSelect:
der Textschriften-Fächer,*
Hermann Schmidt Mainz 2016

Typeface Classifications

British Standards Classification
of Typefaces (BS 2961:1967)

Classification de Maximilien Vox
(NF Q60-007:1977)

DIN Klassifikation der Schriften
(DIN 16518:1964-08)

ISO/IEC 9541-1-2012

Online Sources

www.fontsinuse.com
www.ilovetypography.com
www.typografie.info
www.typographica.org
www.typolexikon.de
and the respective foundries'
websites (see page 396).

Authors' Websites

www.typ-o.eu
www.typo-labor.de

Concept & Editing

Prof. Eva Kubinyi, assisted
by Ivana Baumann.

This publication is based
on the web app www.typ-0.eu
(see page 390). The student
assistants collaborating
on the editing were Marco
Bazelmans, Andreas Blindert,
Robert Franke, and Henry
Monse.

Translation, Proofreading

Dr. Dan Reynolds

First Edition, 10/2025

Product Safety

Publisher: Braun Publishing AG,
Arenenbergstr. 2,
8268 Salenstein, Switzerland
publisher@braun-publishing.ch

EU-Representative: Bookwise
GmbH, Zeppelinstr. 67,
81669 Munich, Germany
info@bookwise.de

Acknowledgements

We would like to thank
Prof. Johannes Bergerhausen,
Fritz Grögel, Thomas Huot-
Marchand, Jérôme Knebusch,
Alisa Nowak, and Dr. Dan
Reynolds for the professional
exchanges we had with them
and the impulses they provided,
as well as Albert-Jan Pool,
who facilitated our exchanges
with the DIN committee
on 'Schriften'.

This publication was made
possible with the support
of the FH Aachen.

ISBN: 978-3-7212-1049-1